ORTHODOX SPIRITUAL LIFE

ORTHODOX
SPIRITUAL LIFE

by
Giorgios I. Mantzarides

Translated by Keith Schram

HOLY CROSS ORTHODOX PRESS
Brookline, Massachusetts 02146

Funds for the publication of this book
have been graciously provided by the
ARCHBISHOP IAKOVOS
Leadership 100 Endowment Fund

© Copyright 1994 by Holy Cross Orthodox Press
Published by Holy Cross Orthodox Press
50 Goddard Avenue
Brookline, Massachusetts 02445

LIBRARY OF CONGRESS CATALOGING–IN–PUBLICATION DATA

Mantzarides, Georgios I.
[Orthodoxos pneumatike zoe. English]
Orthodox spiritual life / by Giorgios I. Mantzarides ; translated
by Keith Schram.
p. cm.
Previoulsy published: c1994.
Includes bibliographical references and index.
ISBN 0-916586-69-3 (pbk.)
1. Spiritual life—Orthodox Eastern Church. 2. Orthodox Eastern
Church—Doctrines. I. Title.
[BX382.M3713   1999]
2148.4'819—dc21   99-27933
                                          CIP

We are indebted to Holy Transfiguration Monastery for permis-
sion to quote from their translation of *The Ascetical Homilies of
Saint Isaac the Syrian* (Boston, 1984), as we are to St. Vladimir's
Seminary Press to quote from their translation of David Ander-
son, *Saint Basil On the Holy Spirit* (Crestwood, 1980), and to Faber
and Faber for permission to quote from thier translation of Saint
Mark the Ascetic in the *Philokalia*, 1 (1979), and from Saint
Maximos the Confessor, *Philokalia*, 2 (1979).

Contents

PROLOGUE

Spiritual life can never be limited or defined. Therefore, the content of a book about the spiritual life is never able to exhaust the subject that its title indicates. In particular, this book does not even attempt to enlarge upon all the themes of Orthodox spiritual life or to exhaust even the most important among them. Its purpose is to constitute an introductory handbook to assist students of theology, and anyone else who is interested, in a first approach to Orthodox spiritual life.

Giorgios I. Mantzarides

oîkos house
or
nómos law

CHAPTER ONE

economos

The Character of Orthodoxy

ecumenical =

As the prophets have seen, as the Apostles have taught, as the Church
has received, as the teachers have set forth in dogmas, as the world
has understood . . . so we believe, so we speak, so we preach.[1]

Orthodoxy is not a particular Christian confession, but has a
general and transtemporal character. Orthodoxy was not created by
abstractions and divisions, but is the single and unified truth. It is
the truth of the Church, the truth of the body of Christ, which is shared
and not divided, which is distributed and unifies. The truth of Orthodoxy is the fact of God's love for mankind; it is the gift of the
divine economy which creates in the faithful a corresponding obligation and a corresponding responsibility: the obligation and the responsibility for peace and unity among them.

In 842, after the whirlwind of the war against the icons, which had brought back in a new form the old christological heresies, the peace and unity of the Church was restored in the life of her members. Thus, God's gift appeared again in the life of the faithful. The fact of the faith appeared once more as a mark of everyday life. Of course, even in the most brilliant period of the Church's history, the weakness of people who belong to her and who are often led into heresies and schisms does not cease to exist. The final triumph of the Church, the appearance of her indissoluble unity, will be realized in the eschaton, when the Church scattered in the world will be gathered into the kingdom of God.[2]

But this does not at all mean to justify our not living unity even now. Unity characterizes the nature of the Church. When we do not live unity, we do not live as members of the Church. The Church is not some human organization in which unity might be deemed useful, but not completely necessary. The Church is the body of Christ, and the body of Christ cannot be understood without unity. Christ is one: his Church is one. In the Creed, we confess our faith "in one, holy, catholic and apostolic Church." The many churches, or rather, the many Christian confessions, are constructions of men and not of God.

For some time, though, the Christian world has ceased to constitute one united community of faithful people, one Church. The faith which the Apostles, the Fathers and the teachers of the undivided Church handed on has not been kept unaltered everywhere. The worship has been broken up, the ethos alienated, the harmony destroyed, the tradition abandoned. Thus, a scandal has been created within the world, a scandal to which no Christian can remain indifferent.

The Orthodox Church is not one among the many churches. The Orthodox Church is the undivided Church of Christ. It is the undivided Church of Christ, not because the Orthodox want it so, but because it has emerged so from the common Christian tradition.

> As the prophets have seen, as the Apostles have taught, as the Church has received, as the teachers have set forth in dogmas, as the world has understood . . . so we believe, so we speak, so we preach . . . . This is the faith of the Apostles, this is the faith of the Fathers; this is the faith of the Orthodox; this faith has established the world.[3]

Orthodox sustained the world, because it was always ecumenical. But it cannot persist as Orthodoxy, if it does not also persist as ecumenical. Orthodoxy is not intolerance. Orthodoxy is not conservatism. Orthodoxy is not status quo. Orthodoxy is not ethnicism. Intolerance exploits Orthodoxy and transforms it into a means of factionalism. Orthodoxy is disproved by intolerance so that its spirit disappears, a spirit of love and conciliation. Therefore, those who are intolerant cannot be Orthodox, however orthodox might be the words which they use. But conservatism can also kill the tradition of Orthodoxy and transform it into an ideology, usually to serve alien purposes. Not even some orthodox regime can be identified with Orthodoxy, which is the living tradition of truth and life. Orthodoxy is neither static nor conservative; but, Orthodoxy is dynamic and traditional. Nor is traditionalism conservatism but creativity; it is not a condition, but life. Finally, Orthodoxy is not some ideology. Emphatically, it is not some ethnic ideology.

Of course, some have often attempted to use Orthodoxy as an ideology. This has been done not only by political leaders who pursued their own goals, but by clergy and by laity. The truth, as well as the freedom which truth offers (cf. Jn 8.32), are weighty matters. Some abandon them easily or replace them with their false idols. It is easy for someone to trade in Orthodoxy, but it is difficult to live it. It is easy to boast of being Orthodox — especially when Orthodoxy happens to be in fashion — and to condemn others as apostates or heretics, but it is difficult to live the truth of Orthodoxy. Therefore, we often forget this truth and project our personal or collective desires and self-interest in its name. Thus, we falsify Orthodoxy much more than those whom we characterize as its enemies. When those whom we characterize as enemies of Orthodoxy judge and condemn our distorted Orthodoxy, instead of turning our glance on ourselves, in order to see our condition and to take care to correct it, we launch missiles at them, thinking that in this way we are fulfilling our obligation to Orthodoxy or even that we are becoming her confessors.

Orthodoxy is not an ideology, but truth and life. It honors the particularity of people, their language, their traditions, their customs. Just as Christ by his incarnation assumed the entire human nature, so also the Church of Christ, the Orthodox Church, assumes everything human within history. But also, as Christ did not assume sin, because this constitutes a condition contrary to nature for man, so also the Church, or better, those who wish to belong to the Church, to the everlasting and indivisible body of Christ, cannot allow states of sin to dominate in our lives and in our relationships. The freedom which Christ grants cannot be used "as a ground for the flesh," but must be revealed by a spirit of love and mutual service (v. Gal 5.13). This freedom is not being unaccountable, but a call to free ourselves completely from the source of sin and division, which is our egoism — and to find in Christ the university of our nature.

In fact, many of the obstacles we meet daily would disappear, if this disposition were in us! How many contradictions would be put aside, if individual or party egoism did not dominate in our relationships! How many divisions would be cancelled, if national or confessional egoism did not prevail in our religious life! "If the salt has lost its taste," says the Lord, "with what will it be salted?" (Mk 9.50) If we Christians, or even if we Orthodox, who boast that we preserve unaltered the truth of Christ, do not take care to work in this direction, on whom are we waiting? The Church continually directs us to the goal of fighting against egoism in its different forms. Repentance, the life work of a Christian, has this same goal in view as well.

Orthodoxy is not some objectified value which someone can use in accord with his tastes and desires. Orthodoxy is not a property of someone who thinks he owns it. No one can own Orthodoxy. He can only be owned by it. No one can enlist Orthodoxy in his schemes in order to condemn or fight others, in order to make or become fanatics. True Orthodoxy (we are not speaking of its falsifications) cannot be enlisted in anything else, but calls everyone to a universal enlistment. Otherwise, even Baptism in the Orthodox Church is nothing else than enrollment in it. The progress of the faithful in the Orthodox Church is realized to the extent that they make their enrollment in it effective, to the extent that they do not let egoism and its consequences dominate in their lives and empty their faith, their hope, and their love, leaving only the appearance of them.

When, then, we fell ourselves to be members of the Orthodox

Church, members of the body of Christ, the divisions of the Christian world cannot be indifferent to us. The pain which these divisions provoke are our own pain. The concern for their elimination must be the concern of us all. But in order to help Christians of other confessions, we do not need to make compromises in our faith. By such compromises we betray both ourselves and them, because they need the Christian truth untainted. For us to help Christians of other confessions, especially now when circumstances bring us very near them, we need to turn to our own roots; we need to know our Orthodoxy better and to seek her universal and ecumenical truth.

With this attitude, for sometime the slogan "back to the Fathers" has been proposed. This cannot be considered absolutely satisfactory, because it could be interpreted also as reactionary. Therefore, the slogan "forward with the Fathers" has been proposed instead. But these slogans do not accurately formulate the position of Orthodoxy. The position of Orthodoxy is: "Following the Holy Fathers."[4] To follow does not mean either to return or to walk forward. To follow means to come after, and the one who comes after does not determine his course by himself, but is set on the course of him or them whom he comes after, "Following the holy Fathers," then, means "Coming after the holy Fathers", not returning to the past of their historical presence, nor transforming them into archeological treasures in the present and future. "Following the holy Fathers" means accepting the living presence of the holy Fathers as members of the single body of Christ, to which we also belong, and being led by their life teaching, by their manner and mind. This is the sole duty of the Orthodox. This duty weights on us all, and especially on us Greeks, who have combined our history with the cultivation and the teaching of ecumenical Orthodoxy. The great Fathers and Ecumenical Teachers demand this of us. The cloud of martyrs and saints of our Church teach us this.

_____

Are they saying this is wrong to do??

Extract from the "Synodicon of Orthodoxy"[5]

As the prophets have seen, as the Apostles have taught, as the Church has received, as the teachers have set forth in dogmas, as the world has understood, as grace has shone forth, as truth has been received, as falsehood has been driven away, as wisdom has freely spoken, as Christ has been the judge; so we speak, so we proclaim Christ our true God, and honor his Saints in words, in writings, in thoughts, in sacrifices, in churches, in images, worshipping him as God and Master, and honoring them because of our common Master as his genuine companions and assigning them relative worship.

This is the faith of the Apostles; this is the faith of the Fathers; this is the faith of the Orthodox; this faith sustains the world.

Moreover, we acclaim the heralds of piety fraternally and agreeably to the Fathers to the glory and honor of the piety for which they struggled and we say:

To Germanos, Tarasios, Nikephoros and Methodios, as being truly high priests of God, champions and teachers of Orthodoxy, eternal memory.

To Ignatios, Photios, Stephanos, Antonios, and Nicholas the most holy and orthodox Patriarchs, eternal memory.

To all that has been written or spoken against the holy Patriarchs Germanos, Tarasios, Nikephoros and Methodios, Ignatios, Photios, Nikephoros, Antonios and Nicholas, anathema.

To all the novelties contrary to the ecclesial tradition and the teaching and formulation of the holy Fathers of blessed memory or that shall be done after this, anathema.

To Arius the first to fight against God and the leader of heresies, anathema.

To Peter the Fuller and madman who said "Holy Immortal One, who was crucified for us," anathema.

To Nestorios who was sent by God's wrath and who said the

Holy Trinity is passible, and to Valentinus the impious mad-man, anathema.

NOTES

[1] *Synodicon of Orthodoxy*, Seventh Ecumenical Council.

[2] Cf. *The Didache* 9,4, *The Apostolic Fathers*, vol. 1, tr. Kirsopp Lake (Cambridge, MA, 1977), p. 322.

[3] *Synodicon of Orthodoxy*, Seventh Ecumenical Council.

[4] The definition of the Chalcedon is introduced with this phrase; see Mansi, 7, 116.

[5] Ibid. 13.813-16.

CHAPTER TWO

The Concept of
the Spiritual Life

obedience to the H.S.

It is usual in our time for there to be discussion among the Orthodox, not only about orthodox spiritual life, but also about Orthodox spirituality. The term "spirituality," which is unknown in the biblical and patristic tradition, derives from western theology, and presents the ethico-religious life of the faithful in opposition to the life of the worldly or of those without faith.[1] In this way, a theological tendency is expressed which, even though it does not characterize itself as an ideology because it is clear that Christianity cannot be reduced to ideology, is not in reality something very different.

Spirituality is an abstract concept which has no place in the tradition of the Orthodox Church. Spirituality is the mother of materialism, together with whatever distorts and dissolves the universality of the truth of Christianity. Therefore, the concept "Orthodox spirituality"

8

must be abandoned. In the tradition of the Orthodox Church, the Spirit is known as a person and as a personal grace. He is the third person of the Holy Trinity and the grace of the Triadic God who is offered to man and makes him spiritual. The Spirit is not some idea. And the spiritual man is not someone with many or with beautiful ideas, with good manners or with high visions. A spiritual man is the man who shares in the grace of God, who is a participant in divine life.[2] Or to express it in Palamite terminology, a spiritual man is a created man who shares in the uncreated grace of God.

"The spiritual man," writes St Gregory Palamas, "is constituted from three things: the grace of the heavenly Spirit, a reasonable soul and an earthly body."[3] Even the body of man becomes spiritual when it shares in the uncreated grace of the Holy Spirit. Likewise, from the other direction, the spirit itself becomes unspiritual and fleshly when it does not share in this uncreated grace.[4] Finally, even the life of man becomes spiritual, when it is directed by the grace of the Holy Spirit. So long as man is confined in his created nature, he cannot have a spiritual life. So long as he relies on his abilities, his knowledge, his virtues, and his vision, he remains fleshly. The spiritual life cannot spring from man. It does not consititute a fruit of the intellectual or moral virtues, nor is it cultivated by emotionalism and calculation. The spiritual life springs from God; it is offered by his grace revealed in Christ and manifest as a fruit of the Holy Spirit.

The spiritual life of man rests on the following basic assumptions:
a) his creation "in the image and likeness" of God,
b) his renewal in Christ and the deification of his nature, and
c) the possibility for him to become a participant in the gift of Christ by the grace of the Holy Spirit.

Man has come from God and his existence portrays him. Being "in the image" constitutes a mark common to all people. But the same cannot be said of being "in the likeness," which is offered to man only as a possibility. But characteristically, St. Gregory Palamas observes, "everyone is in the image of God, perhaps even in the likeness."[5] Likeness to God is not imposed on man by force, but he is left to his free disposition. The fall, as a distancing from God, obscured the "image" and made likeness to God impossible. But the incarnation of the

Word of God renewed and deified human nature. Thus, the way of likeness to God and of deification was again opened to man. The faithful person walks in this way by the grace of the Holy Spirit.

The Holy Spirit does not effect an independent work of renewal, but makes each one a participant in the work of renewal which was completed once for all in Christ. The gift of Christ is offered personally to each person. The deification of human nature becomes also the deification of the several persons, in order that the "communion of deification" be formed. Thus, the Son of God is one with the human nature which he assumed: "For in his hypostasis, he is united with the first fruits of humanity from men."[6] Christ is not united with each of the faithful "in his hypostasis," but "in his energy and grace." Therefore, Christ is and remains one, while the Christlike are many and are made one by the communion of grace of the Holy Spirit.

The Holy Spirit, who proceeds from the Father — and not from the Father and from the Son (*filioque*) — forms the faithful into a communion of persons in the image of the Triadic God. The *filioque*, which has become established in western theology, is a basic dogmatic error, which relates to the core of the faith, the dogma of the Trinity, but with broader ecclesiological and anthropological consequences as well. It is the first characteristic symptom that theology is becoming detached from the life and experience of the Church. That is, while the ecclesial theology is founded on the experience of the presence of God within history, another kind of theology is introduced with the *filioque*. This theology, starting initially from a super-orthodox polemical attitude and trying to found the equality of the Son with the Father on a metaphysical basis, essentially puts aside the person and personal experience and develops by stages into a theology become ideology. Of course, it is not only the theology which is combined with the *filioque* which can be made into ideology.

Even Orthodox theology without the *filioque* and without any other western unorthodoxy can become, and in our days often does become, another form of ideological theology. What is to be noted here about the doctrine of the *filioque* is that this constitutes the first characteristic instance of the transformation of the theology to become established officially over a large part of the Christian world. The establishment

God baptized the water for its use in baptizing us.

of this theological position, which submits the person to the principle of the essence, exhibits in an evolutionary way the widest ecclesiological and anthropological consequences in the submission of the person and the community to the institution and to institutionalized authority.

The formation of the faithful into a community of persons into image of the Triadic God begins with the sacrament of Baptism. Baptism is the birth "from above" by which man's being "in the image" is illuminated and the road is opened to become "in the likeness." In Baptism, the communion of Christ's death and resurrection is offered to man personally. But in order for this communion to be given effect, he must mortify his fleshly life and enlist himself in the life into which he is initiated by the grace of the Holy Spirit, or to recall the words of John the Evangelist, the power which man has received to become a child of God needs to be made effective (see Jn 1.12). Thus, it becomes obvious that the spiritual life of the Christian, which is founded by Baptism, has a dynamic character. *active?*

The grace of Baptism, as St. Diadochos of Photike notes, is established in the depths of the mind from the moment of Baptism, hiding its presence from the mind's awareness. When the faithful begin to love God with their whole will, then in an inexpressible way, this grace offers a portion of its good to the soul with the awareness of the mind. Finally, comparably with the progress of the soul, the grace of God reveals its goodness to the mind.[7] And so, as St Gregory Palamas observes, he who is baptized receives the power to become a son and heir of God, but his full adoption is realized in the kingdom of God, if he preserves in his life his communion with Christ.[8]

The sacrament of Chrismation is connected to the sacrament of Baptism. Thus, while Baptism leads into the life in Christ, Chrismation supplies the energy for the realization of this life. As St Nicholas Kabasilas notes, Chrismation "activates the spiritual energies, one in one man, another in another, or even several at the same time, depending on how each man is prepared for this Mystery."[9]

The organic relationship of these sacraments is also shown by their liturgical combination, which is preserved until today in the Orthodox Church. In the Orthodox liturgical rite, the gift of the Holy Chrism is offered immediately after Baptism.

The third fundamental sacrament, in which the purpose of the two preceding sacraments is fulfilled, is the holy Eucharist.[10] The organic combination of Baptism and Chrismation with the Holy Eucharist is shown again by the liturgical tradition of the Church, as well as by the practice which exists even today among the Orthodox.

In the first centuries of the Church's history, the newly enlightened, immediately after Baptism and Chrismation, were directed to the Divine Liturgy and shared in the Holy Eucharist. Therefore, even until today at the feasts which were dedicated for group baptism of the catachumens (Easter, Pentecost, Christmas, Epiphany, etc.), the hymn "Trisagion" — "Holy God, holy and mighty . . ." — which is sung after the Little Entrance, is replaced by the hymn, "As many as have been baptized into Christ . . . ," which was sung when the newly enlightened came to the Holy Eucharist.[11] But even when, for practical reasons, the Church has separated Baptism from the Divine Liturgy, its connection with the Holy Eucharist has been preserved. St. Nicholas Kabasilas in the second half of the fourteenth century writes, "After the Chrismation we go to the table. This is the perfection of the life in Christ; for those who attain it there is nothing lacking for the blessedness which they see."[12] This principle is still preserved today in the Greek Orthodox Church, while elsewhere a proposal has been formulated for the restoration of the baptismal liturgy.[13]

As they approach the Holy Eucharist, the faithful become of one body and of one blood with Christ and participants in his incorruptible and eternal life. We do not have here, then, some simple moral union, but an ontological reconstruction and renewal. Thus, while Christ is and always remains one, because he has "one entirely indivisible hypostasis," many may be made "in the form of Christ."[14]

But human cooperation is needed for the grace of the sacraments to bear fruit. Without this co-operation, the grace of God remains ineffective in man. Therefore, the faithful are called to invest all their strenghth and to co-operate with the grace of God for their renewal and deification. Moreover, the sacraments are indices of the life in accord with Christ, which constitutes the ethical side of the life in Christ. "For this is the end of baptism," writes St Nicholas Kabasilas, "to imitate the witness of Christ under Pilate and his perseverance until the

cross and death.''[15] And in relation to the Holy Eucharist, St Gregory
Palamas writes:

> The crucified body of Christ, itself present before us for nourishment,
> teaches us these things and, i.e., to avoid sin and to practice virtue;
> therefore, as we are nourished by this, at the same time we are being
> taught to communicate in his virtues and his sufferings, so that we
> may live eternally with him and reign with him.[16]

The sacraments do not transform man magically, but initiate him.
That is, they introduce him to the life of the Holy Spirit's grace. Whoever
receives the grace of the sacraments is called to live and to reveal in
his life the life of Christ. To the extent that man abandons himself to
the grace of God, to the extent that he lives and behaves in accord
with the form of the sacrament, he lives abd progresses spiritually. Man
does not understand at the outset the greatness of the sacrament. But,
however much he might progress in the spiritual life, he cannot live
the life of grace in its fulness, because he is limited by space and time.
In spite of that, man's progress in the spiritual life is unlimited and
is realized in proportion to the progress of his self-offering to the grace
of God. In order for man to live in Christ, in order to be resurrected
with him, he must offer his life to him, to descend with him to hell.
Moreover, even Christ's resurrection is represented in iconography of
the Orthodox Church by his descent into hell.

Man's self-offering to the grace of God does not constitute a denial
of life, but an affirmation of its general transformation which God effects. This does not mean contempt for joy, but a search for the true
joy which cannot be taken away. It does not entail a flight from reality
or limitation to an ephemeral ''spirituality''; but, to the contrary, a
reference to the eternal and indestructible reality which exists behind
a deceptive immediacy. Therefore, the fruit of the Holy Spirit, that is,
the fruit of the presence of God in man, is not self-exclusion, grief, trouble, faint-heartedness and the like, but love, joy, peace, patience, etc.
(cf. Gal 5.22).

Of course, this seems paradoxical to the worldly minded man. It
is natural that it seems paradoxical, because God himself who created,
contains, and sustains all seems paradoxical to the worldly-minded man.

God is nowhere to those who see only with the body, for he is invisible; but he is everywhere for those who perceive by the spirit, for he is present. He is in all and beyond all, and so he is near to those who fear him, but his salvation is far from sinners.[17]

The monk who dies to the world and devotes himself to asceticism and prayer is pursuing nothing more than what every faithful person who lives in the world ought to pursue. But since the world often forgets God and its cares favor forgetting his presence, the monk leaves the world and the concerns of the world and turns without distraction to the recollection of God and the communication of the Holy Spirit. Monasticism is a spiritual service in the life of the Church which became necessary with the secularization of its members. Therefore, a living Christian Church without monasticism is unthinkable, especially in the contemporary secularized community. So much for the question which is proposed, usually from the side of heterodox Christians, about the meaning a socially non-militant monasticism can have. An answer is pointless in among the Orthodox, where the importance of communion with God and the reality of the secularization of the life of the faithful within the world is kept in view. With monasticism as an escort and counsellor, the faithful within the world manage to overcome the obstacles of secular life, to fight against the forgetfulness of and contempt for the will of God which the secular mind cultivates and to live the spiritual life as living members of the Church of Christ.

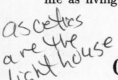

St. John Chrysostom
Commentary on the Letter
to the Romans[18]

"But you are not in the flesh, but in the spirit," he says (Rom 8.9). What then? They were not in the flesh. But did they go around without bodies? How could it have this sense? You see that he alludes to the fleshly life. But why didn't he say, "But you are not is sin?" So that you may learn that Christ has not only extinguished the tyranny of sin, but has also made the flesh lighter and more spiritual, not by changing its nature, but rather by giving it wings. For just as when fire comes into contact with iron the iron also becomes fire while remaining in its proper nature, so it is when the faithful have the Spirit. The flesh, then, changes to that mode of activity, becoming wholly spiritual, being crucified from all sides, and revived by the soul, as was the body of the one who says these things. Therefore, he scorned all luxury and pleasure; he delighted in starvation and flogging and jails. And he did not feel pain in suffering these things. He showed this when he said, "For this light affliction of ours is momentary" (2 Cor 4.17). And so he was well, because he had trained the flesh to concur with the spirit.

"If, indeed, the Spirit of God dwells in you" (Rom 8.9b).

He often uses the expression, "if indeed," as when he says, "if indeed it is just for God to repay those who afflict you with affliction" (2 Thes 1.6); or again, "Did you experience so many things in vain? If it was, indeed, in vain" (Gal 3.4).

"If someone doesn't have the Spirit of Christ"(Rom 8.9b).

He did not say, "If you do not have," but uses the example of the condition that is painful for others. "He is not his," he says (Rom 8.9d).

"If Christ is in you" (Rom 8.10a).

Again, he refers Christ to them. What is painful is short and parenthetical; but, what is desirable brackets it at length so that it is cast in shadow. When he said this, he did not say that the spirit is Christ. Far from it! But he indicated that whoever has the Spirit is not only said to be Christ's, but has Christ himself. For if the Spirit is present, it is not possible that Christ not be present. For wherever one hypostasis of the Trinity is present, the whole Trinity is present. For it is undivided in itself and is united with all precision. What will happen, one might ask, if Christ be in you?

"The body is dead because of sin, but the spirit is life because of righteousness" (Rom 8.10b).

Do you see how many evils come from not having the Holy Spirit? Death, enmity to God, the inability to satisfy his laws, not being Christ's as you ought, not having him dwelling in you. Now look at how many goods come from having the Spirit: belonging to Christ, having Christ himself, emulating the angels. For this is what mortifying the flesh is, to live an immortal life, to have already here the pledges of the resur-

rection, to run the race of virtue with ease. For he did not say that
the body is inactive in sin, but that it is dead, reinforcing the ease of
the race. The one who runs in this way wins the trophy without troubles
and pains. Therefore, he has added "to sin," so that you may learn
that he has cancelled once for all the evil and not the nature of the
body. For if this were the case, many of its possibilities to benefit the
soul would also be cancelled. He does not, though, say this; but living
and remaining, he wishes it to be dead. For this is the sign of having
the Son, of the Spirit being in us, that our bodies differ in no respect
to bodies lying in a coffin with respect to the work of the body.

But don't be afraid when you hear of mortification for you have
the real life which no death will follow. For such life is of the Spirit.
It does not give way, then, to death, but exhausts death and consumes
it. What it has received, it maintains immortal. Therefore, when he said
that the body is dead, he did not say the Spirit is alive, but is life, in
order to show that he is able to grant this to others.Then again, to secure
his hearer he tells him what the cause of life is and also its proof, and
that is righteousness. For where there is no sin, death does not appear;
and where death does not appear, there is indestructible life.

"If the Spirit of the one who raised Jesus from the dead dwells in
you, he who raised the Lord will give life to your mortal bodies also,
through his Spirit dwelling in you"(Rom 8.11).

Again he raises the point of the resurrection, since this hope most
encouraged his hearer, and assured him from what happened to Christ.
Do not, then, be afraid, he says, that you are situated in a dead body.
Possess the Spirit, and it will be raised in any case. What then? Are
bodies which do not have the Spirit not raised? But how is it necessary
for all to stand before the judgement seat of Christ? (v. Rom 14.10)
How trustworthy is the account of Gehenna? For if those who do not
have the Spirit are not raised, nor is there a Gehenna.

What, then, are we to say? All will be raised, but not all to life,
but some to hell and others to life (v. Dan 12.2, Jn 5.29). Therefore,
he did not say, "he will raise,"but, "he will give life." This is more
than the resurrection, and it is to be given only to the just. Positing
the cause of so great an honor, he adds, "through his Spirit dwelling
in you." And so, if you drive away the grace of the Spirit while you

are here and do not depart having it intact, you will surely be destroyed, even if you are resurrected. For as he could not to hand you over to hell if he sees his Spirit shining in you then, so he will not deign to bring you into the bridal chamber if he sees it extinguished, just like those virgins (Mt 25.12).

Don't then, let the body live now, so that it may live then. Make it die, so that it does not die. For if it remains alive, it will not live; but, if it dies, it will then live. And this will in the general resurrection, for first it is necessary to die and be buried, and then to become immortal. and this happens in Baptism. It has, therefore, first been crucified and burried and then raised. And this in the Lord's body. For indeed, that has been crucified and buried and then raised.

NOTES

[1] Cf. O. Höffe, ed., "Spiritualité," *Dictionnaire de Morale* (Paris 1983), pp. 190-91.

[2] St. John Klimakos observes that man is said to be spiritual "from the activity of the Spirit." *De prophetarum obscuritate* 2.5, PG 56.182.

[3] *Triads in Defence of the Holy Hesychasts*, 1.3.43, *Erga* 2.240.

[4] "We have received a body, a creature of God's hands, so that by our return it can become spiritual also, and we by our assent to earthly things have made even our spirit to be flesh. . . ." *Homily*, 43.10. *Erga*, 11.36.

[5] *Letter to Barlaam* 2.48, *Erga* 1.568.

[6] *Against Akindynos* 3.6.13, *Erga* 5.382.

[7] St. Diadochos of Photike, *On Spiritual Knowledge* 77, *Philokalia* 1.279.

[8] *Homilies* 57.16, *Erga* 11.446.

[9] *The Life in Christ* 3.1, p. 103.

[10] "For this is the end of every sacrament, that we being delivered from error and the stain of sin, being made pure and sealed in Christ by the Holy Spirit, may communicate in the body and blood of this Christ, and be united to him in the highest degree." St. Symeon of Thessalonike, *On the Sacred Ceremonies*, 68, PG 155.233B.

[11] Alexander Schmemann, *Of Water and the Spirit*, p. 111. Cf. St. John Chrysostom, *Catecheses*, 2.27. These hymns are, in full, "Holy God, holy and mighty, holy Immortal One, have mercy on us" and "As many of you as have been baptized into Christ have put on Christ. Alleluia.!"

[12] *The Life in Christ* 4, p. 113.

[13] Schmemann, p. 169.

[14] St. Gregory Palamas, *Against Akindynos* 3.6.13, *Erga* 5, 382.

[15] *The Life in Christ* 2, p. 94.

[16] *Homilies* 56.16, *Erga* 11.418.

[17] St. Symeon the New Theologian, *Practical and Theological Chapters* 1, ed. J. Darrouz, *Sources Chrétiennes* 51, Paris 1957, p. 40.

[18] *Homily 13.8*, PG 60.518-20.

CHAPTER THREE

A Religious and Social Nature

Man is not a simple biological unit, but a free person with unlimited depth and breadth, created "in the image and likeness" of God (Gen 1.26). Man's social nature does not constitute an incidental phenomenon, but a characteristic mark of his very nature. Man is a social being, and his social nature does not move only horizontally, but also on the vertical plane. He is not limited only to the sphere of immediacy, but also extends to transcendent dimensions.

The source of man's social nature is the loving or erotic will which he possesses as a creature "in the image and likeness" of God, who is love (v. 1 Jn 4.8). Usually, the concept of love as *agape* is differentiated from the concept of love as *eros*,[1] because the former manifests the disinterested movement of self-offering, while *eros* is the self-interested movement which seeks some satisfaction. Thus, for example, the movement of God toward man is characterized as *agape*, while the movement of man toward God is characterized as *eros*.[1] Man constitutes the object of God's *agape*, whereas God is the object of man's *eros*. But at other times, the two terms are used in exactly the same way as synonyms.

In the Areopagitic writings we read, "Whether we consider eros to be divine, angelic, intellectual, psychic, or natural, we must understand it to be a unifying and binding power which moves superiors to provide for the weaker, which moves equals into a communion with one another. . . ."[2] Here, the word *eros* is used as a synonym for the word love (*agape*).

Eros, then, or love, as "a unifying and binding power," leads man on the one hand to communion with his fellows and on the other to religious reference, that is, to a relationship and communion with God. And so, the social nature of man is not exhausted on the level of his being in the world, but also has a third dimension. In other words, man's social nature is completed and integrated by what we usually characterize as his religious nature. Without the latter, the human social nature degenerates into a fragile conventionality, which has no meaning or content. Man's social relationships and social values fail with time and are finally dissolved by death.

With his religious nature, man seeks the cause of his existence, which he knows is found outside of himself. But when man is moved egoistically, he ends in self-certainty and self-justification, creating a God who constitutes in the final analysis a projection of his generalized and socialized self. He idolizes the values which he creates by his desires and is satisfied with the self-sufficiency which intrigues whithin his illusory and fragile social armor.

This religious nature which, by a movement of self-trancendence and liberation from wordly necessity, is essentially transformed into an attempt at self-justification and self-certainty on the social level, constitutes in reality a repetition of the original sin. Such a religious nature creates, perhaps, even a false sensation of communion with God. But in reality, it refers man back to himself again from another angle.

Man cannot find God by his movement toward him, but by the movement which God makes toward man. The religious nature is a spontaneous human expression which remains, however, in suspense without the response of god. Still more, when the religious nature is accompanied by a false sense of certainty and self-sufficiency, it is changed into an impenetrable barrier which frustrates true communion with God. This truth is formulated epigrammatically by St Paul in his Letter to the Galatians in the following reversal: "Knowing God, or rather, being known by God" (4.9). Knowledge of God is realized, when God makes himself known to man. In this meeting, which happens with the revelation of God to man, the recognition of God's presence is not imposed by force, but is offered as a free choice. Therefore, the sole possibility of man's communion with God is the possibility which faith offers, that is, the possibility of free reference and self-offering.

Man is a living image of God, and it is very natural for a living image to seek out its original. With this seeking, the image preserves its authenticity. Man's inability to stop this search reveals his property as an image of God. Man can never live without his god or gods. the difference is found in the kind of god or gods which he acknowledges. Even atheists have their own gods. But all these gods are created by men and die with men. They are gods who are born within space and decay in time. By contrast, the God of revelation is found beyond space and time.

Between man and God there is a barrier of space and time, which is connected with the createdness of man. After the fall, this barrier translated into a barrier of decay and death. In order for created man to approach the uncreated God, he must cross this barrier, that is, he must die. But when he dies, he is no longer in a position to approach him. Therefore, even the religious reference of man, which is spontaneous and authentic in its beginning, is condemned to fail in the search for God.

Precisely here, the truth of the economy in Christ finds man. God comes in Christ in order to meet man within time and space, that is, within decay and death. Therefore, even man's meeting with Christ is connected with the experience of death. The meeting with Christ is not realized as a result of the religious journey of man, but as an enlightenment on the sea of his failure. There where man approaches the boundaries of despair, there where he sees his longing for fulness and integrity crushed, there where he realizes the absence of God, there also he finds the greatest possibilities for meeting and knowing God. And so it happens that the denial of God often constitutes a phase within man's journey and his searching.

In the final analysis, then, man cannot find God by his religious nature, but by humility. St Symeon the Theodochos,[3] the man of the Presentation is a case in point. Symeon was just and pious throughout his life, but his meeting with Christ was realized when he reached the end of his life with humility and patience, without submitting to his own idols and without becoming disheartened by God's delay. This meeting enabled Symeon to be freed from the fear of death: "Now, Master, release your servant in peace according to your word."

When man meets God and comes into communion with him, he is enabled to conquer the fear of death and to find the meaning of his life beyond it. This communion is not realized on intelligible or transcendent levels, but within the framework of everyday life, in space and time where man moves and acts. And so this communion is not unrelated to the social nature which is expressed on a horizontal plane. To the contrary, rather, communion with God defines by analogy communion with our neighbor.

St. John the Evangelist in his first general Epistle notes briefly the following: "If anyone says, 'I love God,' and hates his brother, he is a liar; for if he does not love his brother whom he can see, how can he love God whom he cannot see?" (1 Jn 4.20) Love for God passes by way of love for one's neighbor; and love for one's neighbor finds its fulness within the light of God's love. St Chrysostom compares the relationship which exists between love for God and love for one's neighbor with the relationship which exists between the soul and the body.[4] The single psychosomatic existence of man is composed of soul and body. His religious and social natures express his deepest nature. They comprise an indissoluble unity, as expressions of his own nature which was created "in the image" of the God of love. This unity is experienced especially in Orthodoxy, where the religious nature is expressed as a vertical social nature and the social as a horizontal religious nature.

God is not some impersonal principle, inaccessible and unapproachable to man, but a Triadic unity of persons, of the Father, of the Son, and of the Holy Spirit. The one and undivided Triadic God comes to a personal communion with men. Man, on the other hand, is not some self-determined individual who can exist and live autonomously, but a person who is conjoined directly with his fellow men, together with whom he forms the image of the one and undivided Triadic God.

When we analyze the concept of being "in the image," we usually define it in persons severally or even locate it in certain of their particular properties, as for instance, in freedom, in the authority to have dominion, in rationality, etc. This is correct, but not enough. In fact, if one begins from the truth of God, it will be understood that the image of God cannot be defined in any individual existence whatever, most simply because God is not himself an individuality, but a Triadic unity. The Word of God, who constitutes the archetype of the creation of man, is one person of the consubstantial and undivided Triadic Divinity. When we seek, then, the image of God in man, we cannot limit ourselves to the individual, but we must extend ourselves to the human community. Further, even man is not a self-enclosed individual, but a person, who exists and lives in relation and with reference to other persons. But the Word of God always exists inseparably with the Father and the Holy Spirit, and so man created in his image always exists in relationship and community with his fellow men.

Man, then, forms the image of God as a person and as a communion of persons. Characteristically St Gregory of Nyssa notes that the whole human nature "extending from the first to the last is one image of being."[5] Of course, between the uncreated Triadic Divinity and the created humanity which exists in many hypostases, there are essential differences. Especially, as St John of Damascus notes, the community and unity of persons in God exists in reality, while in men it is conceived only by reason and reflection. Thus, for example, in God the one nature of the three persons exists in reality with their consubstantiality, while on the level of men it is only with the mind that we consider that Peter and Paul have a common nature.[6]

Each of us, as a creature "in the image and likeness" of God, can contain within himself the entire humanity, just as the persons of the Triadic Divinity who "interpenetrate" one another, each bears the fulness of Divinity. The command of God assumes this and summons man to it: "Love your neighbor as yourself" (Mt 19.19,cf. Lev 19.18). This command shows, in other words, that man can and must embrace every other man in his heart.[7]

The relative and conventional "interpenetration" of persons, which is noted in our social life, is especially marked in the fields of sociology and social psychology. There exists in everyone the ego and ego and the self, that is, the social identity. The ego is the primitive ability to comprehend and to interiorize the roles of others. The self is the interiorized other. The ego is what exists in us from the beginning, the self is created in the course of our social relationships with others. When we are asked to provide some information, we cannot answer correctly if we do not transpose our selves into the position of those who are asking and reply in the way that we would want to receive that information ourselves. The same thing happens in our relationships with others. If we do not interiorize the roles of others, they cannot understand us.[8]

As a creature of God, made with his Word as the archetype, man has the privilege of being in a continuous dialogue with God and with his neighbor. Man summarizes the inner principle (*logoi*) of all beings in the image of God the Word (*Logos*). That is, as the inner principles of beings refer back to and are summarized in the Word of God,[9] so also the inner principles of beings are concentrated and summarized in man in the image of God the Word. Here moreover, the rationality of man reaches its peak. In other words, man is a rational (*logiko*) being, because he is the image of God the Word.[10] His rationality attains its fulness to the extent that it maintains its general reference to God the Word, which exists indivisibly with the Father and the Holy Spirit. This offers man the possibility of developing a dialogue with God the Word, enlisting the entire creation in this dialogue, while at the same time he is united by his nature with all his fellow men, with whom he shares the image of the one Triadic God.

Saint Basil the Great
Longer Rule[11]

Question 3: Concerning love for one's neighbor.

We will continue our inquiry about the commandment that is second in order and in force.

1. We have said previously that the law cultivates and nourishes the potentials within us like seeds. But since we have received the commandment to love our neighbor (Lev 19.18), let us see if we have also the strength from God to fulfil this commandment. Who, then, does not know that man is a peaceful and social animal and not solitary or wild? Nothing, then, is so characteristic of our nature as to have communion with one another, to need one another, and to love our race. The Lord himself has, then, given us the seeds for these deeds and in consequence demands their fruits, when he says, "I give you a new command, to love one another" (Jn 13.34). Since he wished to urge our souls to carry out this command, he did not seek signs and wonderful works in order to prove that we are his disciples (even though he did grant the power for these through he Holy Spirit); but what did he say? "By this all will know that you are my disciples, if you have love among yourselves" (Jn 13.35). The Lord always combines these commands in this way, so that he refers to himself good works done to our neighbor. Therefore he says, "I hungered and you gave me to eat, etc." (Mt 25.35), and then he adds, "In so much as you have done to one of these the least of my brothers, you have done it to me"(Mt 25.40).

2. Consequently, it is possible for someone to fulfill the second command with the first; with the second, he can return to the first. If someone loves the Lord, he loves his neighbor in consequence, because "whoever loves me," said the Lord, "will keep my commands" (Jn 14.23) and "this is my command, that you love one another, just as I have loved you" (Jn 15.12). Again, if someone loves his neighbor, he pays in full the love due to God, because God receives the kindness as being rendered to himself. For this reason Moses, the faithful servant of God, showed such great love for his brothers, that he preferred that his name be struck from the book of God in

which it was written, if the people were not to be forgiven their sin (Ex 32.32). Paul dared to pray to be cut off from Christ on behalf of his brothers, his kin, wishing to become himself an exchange for the salvation of all in imitation of the Lord (see Rom 9.3). At the same time, he knew that it was impossible for someone to be alienated from God, who would sacrifice God's grace for love of him, intending to keep the greatest of the commandments, and that by this act he would enjoy what he was offering much more. From what has been said, then, it has obviously been proved that the saints attained this measure of love for their neighbor.

NOTES

[1] E.g. Saint Ignatios of Antioch, *To the Romans* 7.2: "My *eros* has been crucified."

[2] *On the Divine Names* 4.15, tr. John D. Jones (Milwaukee, 1980), p. 147; PG 3.713AB.

[3] "Theodochos" — "who received God"; Symeon is called this because he carried Christ in his arms into the temple; see Lk 2.29-32. — tr.

[4] *On Love* PG 60.773-4.

[5] *On the Making of Man* 5, PG 44.185CD.

[6] See *On the Orthodox Faith* 1.8, PG 94.828A.

[7] Archimandrite Sophrony, *The Monk of Mt Athos* (Crestwood, 1975), p. 64.

[8] See A. Zijderveld, *Die abstrakte Gesellschaft* (Frankfurt, 1972), p. 30.

[9] "All things were created through him and for him" (Col 1.16).

[10] "Reason (*logos*) has been given to us, then, in the image of the Word (*Logos*), for [we are called] rational from the Word, who is without beginning, the uncreated, the incomprehensible, my God." Saint Symeon the New Theologian, *Hymns* 44.30-33, Sources Chrétiennes 196 (Paris, 1973), p. 72.

[11] *Regulae fusius tractatae*, PG 31.916A-17D.

citizens of a city that has yet to come

mind body & soul } need a balance

CHAPTER FOUR

Self-knowledge and Knowledge of God

The greatest science for man, writes Clement of Alexandria, is to know himself, because if he knows himself, he will know God.[1] Saint Isaac the Syrian observes: "When a man knows himself, the knowledge of all things is granted to him, for to know one's self is the fulness of the knowledge of all things."[2] Without knowledge of one's self, any other knowledge remains detached and without purpose. But when man knows himself, he recognizes the nature, the limits and the possibilities of his existence, and he can locate himself correctly before God, his neighbor and his own self.

If he knows himself, man understands above all that he is not the cause of his own existence. And so, he is led to seek the cause of his existence, which means the same thing as to seek God. The first motives, then, and the first possibilities for approaching God

26

are in man himself. The way which leads to God, as Saint Athanasios the Great observes, is not far from us or outside of us, but within our own existence. "It is possible to find the beginning within us, as Moses taught when he said, 'The word of faith is in your heart.' "[3] And so, knowledge of self leads to knowledge of God, while knowledge of God reinforces knowledge of self as well.

Man, though, is in a state of fallenness and corruption, which has been inaugurated by original sin. Original sin is not some isolated sin of our ancestors with legal consequences for us, but a sin which was committed by our ancestors and is repeated by all of us in our own existence with our personal sins which alienate and corrupt us. It is the sickness into which man fell at the instigation of the devil, and which the whole human race inherits as decay and death. This sickness is also passed on at the level of social life with the socialization of man, that is, with his inclusion in the human community. As sociology informs us, within the unbroken series of human generations, each of us creates his identity by interiorizing others. Thus, he is united with the human community and shares in original sin with his personal sins. In this way as well, social evil is conjoined with and fed by each person.

Each person interiorizes other people within himself. His reaction to others is a reaction to his own interiorizations. So also, his severance from others is an interior severance, just as his severance from God is both an interior severance and simultaneously a severance from his fellow man. Therefore as well, the salvation of man lies essentially in eliminating this severance and in restoring him as a creation "in the image and likeness" of God (Gen 1.26). Here also is found the purpose of the incarnation. Saint Maximos the Confessor observes characteristically the following:

> In his love for man God became man so that he might unite human nature to himself and stop it from acting evilly towards itself, or rather from being at strife and divided against itself, and from having no rest because of the instability of its will and purpose.[4]

The mind of man, where the Father of the Church especially

distinguished the "image" in his nature, cannot be understood without God. Every image reveals a relationship with what it portrays or a reference to it. Man, too, as a creation "in the image" of God exists in relationship and reference to God. When someone denies God, he is not making some logical mistake. In any case, it is natural for man to make logical mistakes. But when he denies God, above all he is denying his own self, he denies his mind. It is for this reason that the Scripture says, "The fool has said in his heart, there is no God" (Ps 13.1). This foolishness is not a matter of his thoughts, but of man's more general situation and position. It is a matter of the purity and orientation of his mind, of his existence. When the mind of man, where God is imaged, is darkened and ceases to have a relationship with God, he abolishes his own self; he becomes foolish — as foolish as a picture without content. This is the fall of man, his alienation:

> For, when the mind stands apart from God, it becomes animal-like or demon-like and rebels against the limits of its nature, it desires other limits and it does not know what it is to satisfy this greed. It makes itself addicted to its desires, and does not know moderation in pleasure.[5]

Man does not reach this alienation suddenly, but progressively, driven by his conceit. Pursuing comfort and pleasure and fleeing from pain and suffering, he cultivates the various passions which pervert his nature and alienate his personal and social life:

> Thus because in our self-love we pursue pleasure, and because — also out of self-love — we try to escape pain, we generate untold corrupting passions in ourselves.[6]

This situation, in which fallen man finds himself, is usually considered as natural. But in reality it is a question of a perversion or situation "contrary to nature." Therefore, someone who finds himself in this situation is master neither of himself nor, or course, of the world in which he lives. Man's authority to have dominion, which constitutes an expression of his creation "in the image" of God, is left a shell. His social relationships, which constitute another expression of his kinship with the Triadic God, are alienated. No exit from this condition is at all possible without man's return to his own self.

When man does return to himself, he confirms his own weakness. But this return is not some simple intellectual matter, but the most profound existential event which must be realized in the struggle against the passions, in asceticism and concentration within oneself. Since the passions alienate man and enslave him to the world if he does not struggle against them, he is unable to become free and to find himself again. Still, the faithful must devote himself to the practice of virtue and to concentration within himself, so that the grace of God can visit him. Even the various temptations are useful here, because they lead man to the fullest consciousness of his weakness and of the greatness of God.[7]

Monasticism has always used asceticism and concentration within oneself to accomplish its goal, Stillness, which has constituted a basic quest of monks from the beginning — especially within Orthodoxy — favors the realization of this goal. The monk, withdrawing into stillness and there watching over himself, manages to attain a higher degree of knowledge of himself, to fight his passions more radically, and to purify his heart from them in order to be permitted to see God.

Concentration within oneself and knowledge of self acquire in the Church an entirely new content, unknown to the pre-Christian or non-Christian world. Man finds in himself not only his fallen nature, which he tries to cleanse of the passions and the stain of sin, but also the image of God. Still more, the Christian finds in himself the same God who became man and united himself to men. Through the sacraments of the Church, especially in Baptism, Chrismation and the Holy Eucharist, Christ himself comes and dwells in man. And so the birth of Christ, which happened but once from the Blessed Virgin, is mystically repeated in the heart of each of the faithful. Saint Maximos the Confessior writes:

> The divine Logos who once for all was born in the flesh, always in his compassion desires to be born in spirit in those who desire him.

He becomes an infant and moulds himself in them through the virtues. He reveals as much of himself as he knows the recipient can accept.[8]

The faithful person takes the place of the Blessed Virgin spiritually and offers himself so that Christ may be born and formed within his existence. This birth and growth of Christ within him is his own spiritual birth and growth (cf Gal 4.19). Therefore, the person of the Blessed Virgin in the Orthodox tradition constitutes the most perfect example of spiritual exaltation toward God.

And so, the Christian who watches over himself and knows his reborn existence in Christ, knows God himself, who became man and dwelt among men: "And my dwelling shall be in them, and I shall be their God, and they shall be my people" (Ezek 37.27). The glory of God, which in the past overshadowed his chosen people, already illuminates Christians from within their own existence. The light of the Transfiguration, which the disciples of the Lord saw on Mt Tabor, is also seen by the saints of the Church, those who have the requisite purity of the heart. But while at the Transfiguration the body of Christ, which constitutes the source of the divine light, illuminated "from without" those who had been chosen, now this same body, that "has been united to us and is within us, rationally illuminates the soul from within."[9] It is on this basis that orthodox monks support the possibility of seeing the uncreated light of God even in the present life. A possibility which, with many struggles, is held open until today in the Orthodox Church.

Man's return into himself is also a return to God.[10] But the return to God is, in the final analysis, the reception of God who comes and visits man created in his image within his own existence: "Behold, I am standing at the door knocking; if anyone hears my voice and opens the door, I will come in to him and dine with him and he with me" (Rev 3.20).

With the coming of Christ into the world, a new period of life began for the world. Man no longer remains just a creature of God — even if the most perfect — but he acquires the power to become his child: "As many as received him, to them he gave the power to become children of God" (Jn 1.12). The man who "receives" the Son of God and maintains him within becomes himself a son of God by grace. Therefore, the body of a Christian is a temple of the Holy Spirit whom he has from God (see 1 Cor 6.19). The Spirit of the Son of God who cries out in the hearts of men, "Abba, Father" (Gal 4.6), restores their forgotten relationship with God the Father. Only he who receives the Son also receives the Father.

Man's return to God the Father becomes possible, then, by the gift of adoption in Christ. Christ, who as Son of God manifests God the Father in the world, simultaneously assumes men into his own body and makes them sons of his own Father by grace. This adoption does not constitute a juridical act but an empirical event, which is realized by the grace of the Holy Spirit. It does not exist as a theoretical concept, but as a real state. The Fathers of the Church often stress the empirical character of man's adoption and renewal in Christ. Saint Symeon the New Theologian, in particular, emphatically underlines that no one can live in Christ without having at the same time experience of the presence of Christ within him. This experience, indeed, which is always in proportion to the purity of heart of the faithful, constitutes the condition for participation in the heavenly kingdom.[11] Thus the relationship of sonship and fatherhood, which exists between the Son and the Father, by the gift of Christ is extended to the relationship of each one with God the Father. No one knows the Father, "except the Son and he to whom the Son wills to reveal him" (Mt 11.27). The self-knowledge which leads man to knowledge of God, is granted in Christ by adoption and participation in the life of God.

Saint Isaac the Syrian
Homily 8[12]

Blessed is the man who knows his own weakness, because this knowledge becomes to him the foundation, the root, and the beginning of all goodness. For whenever a man learns and truly perceives his own weakness, at that moment he contracts his soul on every side from the laxity that dims knowledge, and he treasures up watchfulness in himself. But no one can perceive his own infirmity if he is not allowed to be tempted a little, either by things that oppress his body, or his soul. For then, comparing his own weakness with God's help, he will straightway understand the greatness of the latter. And again, whenever he looks over the multitude of his devisings, and his wakefulness, his abstinence, the sheltering, and the hedging about of his soul by which he hopes to find assurance for her, and yet sees that he has not obtained it, or again, if his heart has no calm because of his fear and trembling: then at that moment let him understand, and let him know that this fear of his heart shows and reflects that he is altogether in need of some other help. For the heart testifies inwardly, and reflects the lack of something by the fear which strikes and wrestles within it. And because of this, it is confounded, since it is not able to abide in a state of surety; for God's help, he says, is the help that saves. When a man knows that he is in need of Divine help, he makes many prayers. And by as much as he multiplies them, his heart is humbled, for there is no man who will not be humbled when he is making supplication and entreaty. 'A heart that is broken and humbled, God will not despise.' (Ps 50.17) Therefore, as long as the heart is not humbled, it cannot cease from wandering; for humility collects the heart.

But when a man becomes humble, at once mercy encircles him, and then his heart is aware of Divine help, because it finds a certain power and assurance moving in itself. And when a man perceives the coming of Divine help, and that it is this which aids him, then at once his heart is filled with faith, and he understands from this that prayer is the refuge of help, a source of salvation, a treasury of assurance, a haven that rescues from the tempest, a light to those who are in darkness, a staff of the infirm, a shelter in time of temptations, a medicine at the height of sickness, a shield of deliverance in war, an arrow sharpened against the face of his enemies, and, to speak simply: the entire multitude of these good things is found to have its entrance through prayer. From this time forward he revels in the prayer of faith, his heart glistens with clear assurance, and does not continue in its former blindness and the mere speech of the tongue. When he thus perceives these things, he will acquire prayer in his soul, like some treasure. And from his great gladness the form of prayer is turned into shouts of thanksgiving. This is the very thing pronounced by one who has defined the form proper to each of our actions: 'Prayer is joy that sends up thanksgiving.' Here he speaks of the prayer that is achieved through the knowledge of God, that is, prayer that has been sent from God. For at that moment a man does not pray with labor and weariness (as in the rest of his prayer, which is prayed before the experiencing of this grace), and because his heart is full of joy and wonder, it continually wells up motions of confession and gratitude while he silently bows the knee. Nay, from his vehement inner ardour, since he is very greatly moved by astonishment at this comprehension of God's graces, he suddenly raises his voice in praise and glorification of Him, and sends up thanksgiving; and he moves his tongue while being held with great awe.

If any man has reached this in truth and not in fancy, and has made many observations of this reality in himself, and has come to know its many differences by reason of his great experience, he knows what I say, for there is nothing here contrary to the truth. And from this time forward let him cease from pondering vanities, and let him remain with God by means of unbroken prayer while being in anxiety and trepidation lest he be deprived of the magnitude of God's succour.

NOTES

[1] *Paidagogue* 3.1.1. PG 8.556A.

[2] *Homily* 36, p. 162.

[3] *Against the Greeks* 30, PG 25.60D. cf. Dt 30.14.

[4] *Various Texts* 1.47, *Philokalia* 2, 174.

[5] Saint Gregory Palamas, *Homily* 51.10, *Erga* 11,226.

[6] *Various Texts* 53, *Philokalia* 2, 175.

[7] Saint Isaac the Syrian, *Homily* 8, p. 67.

[8] *Various Texts* 1.8, *Philokalia* 2, 165.

[9] Saint Gregory Palamas, *Triads in Defence of the Holy Hesychasts* 1.3.38, *Erga* 2, 230.

[10] "It is said that he who does not first re-integrate himself with his own being by rejecting those passions which are contrary to nature will not be reintegrated

with the Cause of his being — that is, with God — by acquiring supranatural blessings through grace." *Various Texts* 2.40, *Philokalia* 2, 196.

[11]See his *On Those Who Think That They Have the Holy Spirit in Them in an Unknown Way*. J. Darrouzès (ed.), Syméon le Nouveau Théologien, *Traités théologiques et éthiques*, Sources Chrétiennes 129 (Paris 1967).

[12]*The Ascetical Homilies of Saint Isaac the Syrian*, Holy Transfiguration Monastery, Boston 1984, pp. 67-8. The text is reproduced with the exception of the footnotes and the brackets indicating Syriac passages not included in the Greek text.

CHAPTER FIVE

Sin and Repentance

Christians often view sin as the transgression of the chiefly negative commands of the Decalogue: "Do not murder. Do not commit adultery. Do not steal. Do not testify falsely." When someone obeys these commands, he believes that he has all the qualifications to consider himself as a good Christian. Especially when he keeps the seventh commandment faithfully and guards himself from the so-called sins of the flesh, he thinks that he has climbed to the peak of spiritual perfection. If this man is indifferent to Christian love, which constitutes the essence of the Christian proclamation, if he is ignorant of what gentleness or humility mean, he considers that this is of secondary or even of no importance. The Decalogue of the Old Testament, in combination with the innate ethical law which exists in the hearts of men, is considered to be the alpha and omega of Christian life. But the facts cannot be judged so superficially. Therefore, a deeper examination of biblical and patristic teaching is necessary to approach the meaning of sin.

The essence of sin according to the Old Testament is found in man's disposition to ignore God and to put himself in God's place. The most subtle description of sin is offered in the book of Genesis with the account of the fall of the first-formed people. In the New Testament and the patristic tradition, the essence of sin is not different but takes a clearer form. Here, sin is the refusal of man to accept the Gospel of Christ and to live as a member of his Church. Sin is not limited to the isolated deeds, thoughts, activities or desires of man, but is a more general condition which is revealed by all of these, but without being exhausted by them.

In order to understand the essence of sin better, we must see what liberation from it is, what the salvation is which Christ offers to man. The man who lives in sin is a slave of decay and death. His deeds, his thoughts, his activities and his desires are defined by self-interest. He is not in a position to open his heart in order to have room for others, to love them, to see them as images of God, who is the Creator and the source of life for all men. Decay and death are sinful conditions, to which man is enslaved, when he loses his communion with God, the source of life.

As Saint Basil the Great characteristically observes, so far as man "stands apart from life, so far he approaches death. For God is life; the lack of life is death."[1] The price of sin is death, which death is above all separation from God. Bodily death, which comes as a consequence of this primeval death, constitutes essentially an act of God's kindness to man, "lest he preserve immortal the sickness in us."[2] When man distances himself from God, he finds himself under the power of death. And when he is rejoined with God in Christ, he is made a victor over death with him.

Man's salvation consists in his assumption in the body of Christ and his becoming able to live as a victor over decay and death within the light of the resurrection. Christ, as perfect God and perfect man, is the only one who can unite man with God and offer him the life of which he was deprived. Therefore, as well, faith in Christ constitutes the necessary condition for man's salvation.

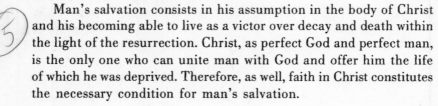

The Gospel, as is easily confirmed, does not divide men according to their virtues or vices, but according to their disposition either to repent or to persist in sin. Christ did not call man to become more virtuous or less sinful, but to repent and to accept the grace which he offers them. In so far as men do not repent, they are far from the true source of their life and are slaves of decay and death. There are no exceptions in this matter: "For all have sinned and come short of the glory of God" (Rom 3.23). Only the consciousness of this reality gives man the measure of his real morality and of his relationship with God. Therefore, it is not at all paradoxical that those who accepted the Gospel of Christ were not the scribes and Pharisees who boasted of their virtues, but the tax-collectors and prostitutes who realized their sinfulness and repented.

Precisely this truth is expressed in the words of Christ to the priest and teachers of the Jews: "Amen, I tell you the tax-collectors and prostitutes precede you into the kingdom of God" (Mt 21.31). Giving this priority to tax-collectors and prostitutes, who were without a doubt the most unethical and iniquitous people of their community, does not mean rewarding immorality and iniquity; even more, it does not mean disapproval of righteousness and virtue. This priority means the affirmation of the general pardon which God offers to the man who repents in fact, to the man who understands his unworthiness and invokes the mercy of God.

When Christ visited Zachaeos, the tax-collector, in his house, he did not do it in order to justify his iniquities, but in order to reward his repentance. When he refused to condemn the woman who was arrested "in the very act of adultery" (Jn 8.5), he did not do it to justify adultery, but in order to manifest the universality of sin and the necessity of repentance for all without exception. Therefore, when the scribes and the Pharisees insisted that Christ judge and condemn the adulteress, he said, "Let the one among you who is without sin first cast a stone at her" (Jn 8.7). And when, one by one, they all withdrew, "one by one, beginning with the elders," Christ said to the woman "Go and from now on, do not sin again" (Jn 8.11).

The secret of man's virtue, according to Christian teaching, is found in the decision to repent. Whoever feels sin weighing on him will take this decision, and conversely, whoever is proud of his virtues will not repent but will remain far from the grace of God. For this reason, sinners are farther ahead of the just on the road to the kingdom of God.

This priority seems odd in the eyes of many. It seems odd, if not unacceptable, even in the eyes of many Christians, regardless of the fact that it was confirmed by Christ himself. This is quite natural, when Christianity is confronted as an ethical teaching, and Christ as a moral teacher, who came to establish righteousness and virtue, as men perceive them. But reading the Gospel, one notices that all human values are essentially put aside or even overturned. Men are not evaluated in accordance with their moral reputation, nor do their social position and dignity give the measure of their worth. The only fixed criterion, the only measure with which to evaluate them is repentance. If man repents, he becomes acceptable in the kingdom of God — he is saved. If he does not repent, whatever else he may do is, finally, useless — it does not save him. This is the Christian criterion. This is the measure by which God judges man.

Indeed, what can the moral quality be, even of the best man, before the holiness of God? What can the value of his virtue be before divine virtue? "All our righteousness is like a polluted rag," says the prophet Isaiah (64.6). Perhaps the thief who inherited Paradise was preferred by Christ because of his virtues?

Of course, it is natural for everyone who repents and believes in Christ to be concerned to cultivate virtue. But who can claim that he serves only virtue and does not sin? Indeed, especially in our days, ethical debauchery has proceeded so far and sin has spread so much that many not only consider it perfectly natural, but even boast about it. The greatest frauds and the most fearful crimes often happen in the most natural manner. It is enough for someone to leave his conscience a little loose in order to reach — without understanding how — disgraceful deeds. Therefore, many Christians feel content with an imperfect spiritual life and forget the tragedy of sin.

However, as Christ himself said, "The strong do not need a doctor, but those who are sick" (Mt 9.12). Insofar as people are concerned to appear moral and correct in society, they are deceived by the illusion of their superficial apperance and forgetful of their deepest selves. They hide not only from society, but also from their own selves, the sickness that is within them and feel contented and strong. They classify themselves among the "strong," among those, that is, who think that they are healthy and "do not need a doctor." But in reality, they are the sick who, precisely because they forget that they are sick, do not think of the doctor and treatment. On the contrary, "those who are sick," those, that is, who have a sense of their sickness, can at least seek the doctor and their cure. The lack of moral self-sufficiency, the absence of superficial worldliness and piety create the conditions for repentance which constitutes man's only possibility of salvation. Therefore, the road of repentance is very near today, if we take cognizance of our condition. It is the road to which the very data of life lead. The data of undisguised sin, of moral decline and spiritual incoherence.

The ethical and spiritual crisis of our age, the expansion and excess of sin do not at all mean the triumph of evil, but rather the expression of its desperate struggle. Evil is not a position, but a denial. It is not an existence, but non-existence. Man proves this empirically by the disruption and nausea, which evil creates within him. And he is delivered from evil as he proceeds from the sense of disruption and nausea to the taste of a repentance which is not a momentary act, nor even an act repeated at definite or indefinite temporal intervals, the taste of a repentance which is a way of life, because the Christian life is a life of repentance.

Sermon 6 of the Monk Damaskinos

"On Repentance" (Extract)[3]

I want to relate, by your love, what kind of thing repentance is, and how man ought to do it, if he wishes God to remit his sins. Every Christian who fears God ought to repent of the evil which he has done and do it no more. There is nothing else greater than repentance, since repentance saved the tax-collector, the prostitute, the thief, David, Paul who previously was a persecutor of Christ but

repented and became the Apostle. What except repentance saved Saint
Mary of Egypt who was a prostitute and adultress? All the Apostles
constantly preached repentance; and John cries: "Repent, for the
kingdom of heaven is near" (Mt 3.2).

But what is this repentance? Listen. Whenever a man does any
evil but wishes to be saved, he is not saved, if he does not leave evil,
and repent of it with all his soul and with all his heart, crying within
himself saying: "I have sinned, my Lord, before heaven and before
you, and I am not worthy to be called your son. Treat me as one of
your hired men" (Lk 15.18-19). So the prodigal son repented, when
he had wasted all his father's property on prostitutes and drunken-
ness and in every other debauchery. Then he thought about it and
said: "Woe to me, the miserable one, how many of my father's hired
men have more than enough bread, and take delight in his goods,
while I am perishing of starvation? (Lk 15.17) Ah, may I return to
my compassionate father, and he will want to receive me, because
he is compassionate. If he just puts it in mind, God will straightway
have mercy, and forgive him his sins.

Saint Mary was a prostitute, and from twelve years old she fell
into sin, and worked in the brothel for seventeen years. One day she
saw that people were going down from Alexandria to Jerusalem, in
order to venerate the honorable and life-giving Cross, because it was
the feast of the Exaltation of the Cross, and she went down to the
boat, and said to the sailors: "Will you take me as well to venerate?"
And the sailors said to her, "If you have the money to pay your fare
and your expreses, nothing prevents you from coming." She said to
them, "I do not have the fare, but I have a beautiful body, as you
see, and you can do whatever you want with it." When the sailors
heard what she said, they rejoiced, because they were full of satanic
lust through and through. They took her into the boat, and what they
did in the boat, who will tell it? Shortly, was there anyone left whom
she had not polluted?

And when she came to Jerusalem, she went to the temple where
the tomb of our Lord Jesus Christ is. All were going in and worship-
ing, but she was invisibly prevented and could not venerate. And she
tried two, three, and even more times, and she could not venerate

at all. There where she stands outside the door, she sees the image
of the most pure Mary, Mother of God, and she remembers the sins
which she has committed. It came into her mind, that her sins
prevented her and she could not venerate in the Church, and
straightaway she repented, and cried with all her soul, saying to the
icon of the Mother of God: "O Lady and Mother of God, who gave
birth to the Son and Word of God, I beg you, give me such grace
that I can venerate within the Church, that even I may worship the
venerable Cross. And I give you my bond, that I will commit sin no
more."

When she finished the prayer, she tried to venerate, and she
venerated without hindrance, when no-one obstructed her; and so she
worshiped, and came out, and went into the desert, and was saved.

You see, brothers, what repentance is like? She spoke only a word
before the icon of our most pure Mother and Lady and Mother of
God, and straightaway her sins were remitted. In the same way it
happens, my brothers, that we must act, to repent with all our soul.

NOTES

[1] *That God Is Not the Cause of Evil*, 7, PG 31.345A.

[2] Ibid. cf. also Theophilos of Antioch, *To Autolykos* 2.26, ed. G. Bardy, Sources
Chrétiennes 20 and Saint Irenaios, *Against Heresies* 3.23.5-6.

[3] Translated from the *Treasury of Damaskinos the Subdeacon and Studies of
Thessalonike*, ed. B. Rigopoulos (Thessalonike, 1971), p. 563-65.

CHAPTER SIX

The Dogmas of the Church
as Pointers to Life

In a synodical text of the Orthodox Church, the following is noted:

> The dogmas previously admitted, commonly known to all and open-
> ly preached were mysteries of the Law of Moses and forseen only
> by the prophets in the Spirit; but the good things promised to the
> saints in the future age are mysteries of the way of life of the Gospel,
> given and forseen by those made worthy through the Spirit to see
> in measure and as in part a pledge.[1]

There is, then, a selective procedure in the revelation of God's
economy in history. This economy begins with the revelation of the
Word of God in the Old Testament before his taking flesh and is
completed by the incarnation in the New Testament in order to be

consummated in the future age, "when Christ will be revealed" (Col 3.4). The entire work of the divine economy is realized by Christ and the whole dogmatic teaching of the Church about the work of the divine economy is summarized in the phrase, "Jesus is the Christ" (v. 1 Jn 5.1). This is the primitive truth of the Church. The dogmas constitute prismatic refractions of the truth that the historical person of Jesus is the promised and awaited Messiah or Christ.

Saint Basil the Great observes that "Christ's name is the confession of everything, for, that is, it reveals the God who anoints, the Son who is anointed, and the Spirit who is the ointment."[2] The Triadic God is revealed in the person of Christ and the confession of Christ is a confession of the Triadic God, who is revealed in history in order to renew and deify man.

In the ecclesial Tradition, theology is usually distinguished from the divine economy. Theology refers to the Triadic God, while the economy to his saving manifestation in the world, Christ, the second person of the Holy Trinity, is the one who "unites the whole economy in one spiritual union."[3]

The work of the divine economy begins with the creation which was realized by the Word of God and is completed with the renewal of the world and the deification of man, to whom is addressed the work of the divine economy, is related responsively to God by theology and the economy.[4] He belives the theology and imitates the economy.[5]

The basic dogmas of the Church are those concerned with the Trinity and with Christ. The doctrine of the Church is an extention and farming of christological dogma. Looking at these dogmas in relation to the primitive truth that "Jesus is the Christ," we can say that the dogma of the Trinity is the theological dimension of this truth, while the christological dogma is its economic dimension. These dogmas cannot be considered as abstract theological concepts, but as truths which critically concern man and his life.

The truth that Jesus is the Christ is not imposed by necessity on man. But on the other hand, man is not in a position by himself to know and confess this truth. "No one can say that Jesus is Lord except by the Holy Spirit" (1 Cor 12.3). The truth about Christ is prepared pedagogically and revealed by the grace of the Holy Spirit. The disciples themselves of Christ after a lengthy acquaintance and communication with him were asked, "Who do men say that the Son of man is?" and "Who do you say that I am?" (Mt 16.13-15) Then Peter replies and says, "You are the Christ, the Son of the living God" (Mt 16.16). This answer, as Christ shows in what follows, is a fruit of God's enlightening: "You are blessed, Simon son of Jonah, because flesh and blood did not reveal this to you, but my Father who is in heaven" (Mt 16.17). The awareness and confession of Christ is not a human work, but a fruit of divine enlightenment. The will and the interest of Peter and of the disciples to know Christ would have remained fruitless without God's enlightenment. But the enlightenment of God remains ineffective without human cooperation. Man's cooperation is expressed by his will to know Christ and by his care to fulfil this will. The will is not enough by itself. It needs care and effort in addition. Time must be devoted to it, a life spent on it. Human cooperation is expressed in this way. But together with human cooperation, divine enlightenment is also required.

Divine enlightenment is offered to man with Baptism, which according to the tradition of the Orthodox Church is combined immediately with Chrismation. Baptism grafts man into the body of Christ, making him a participant in his death and resurrection. Baptism is enrolment in the new life, in the life of Christ. The rite of Baptism, the threefold immersion in the water, indicates the character of the new life. Baptism, then, is not only a sacrament, but a sacramental way of life which unfolds by the continuous participation of the faithful in the death and resurrection of Christ. The whole life of the faithful is essentially a baptism. The true Christian continously dies and lives in Christ. The more intensely he dies, the more intensely he lives in Christ.

As Christ did, so the faithful as members of his body live this dying within the world:

> As that perceptible body of Jesus was crucified, buried and afterwards raised, so the whole body of the saints of Christ has been crucified with Christ and now lives no longer; for each of them,

like Paul, boasts in nothing else except in the cross of our Lord Christ Jesus, through whom he has been crucified to the world and the world to him. Not only, then, has he been crucified with Christ and crucified to the world, but he has also been buried with Christ. For Paul says, "We have been buried with Christ." And just as if he has received some pledge of the resurrection, he says, "We have been raised with him," since he walks in a certain community of life, as one yet raised in accord with the blessing hoped for the final resurrection.[6]

The force which moves Christian in life is the grace of the Holy Spirit, which he is granted with Chrismation immediately after Baptism. As Saint Nicholas Kabasilas notes characteristically,

Baptism confers being and in short, existence according to Christ ... The anointing with chrism perfects him who has received [new] birth by infusing into him the energy that befits such a life.[7]

Finally, the nourishment which sustains the faithful in the life in Christ is the Holy Eucharist. During the first centuries of the Church's history, the newly baptized were directed immediately after Baptism and Chrismation to the Divine Liturgy and participated in the Holy Eucharist. Even late, when the Church for practical reasons detached Baptism and Chrismation from the Divine Liturgy, their connection with the Holy Eucharist was maintained. Saint Nicholas Kabasilas writes:

After the Chrismation we go to the table. This is the perfection of the life in Christ; for those who attain it there is nothing lacking for the blessedness which they seek.[8]

The Holy Eucharist, and Baptism as well, not only nourishes but also indicates to the faithful the new way of life which they are called to live: "For as we are fed by him we are at the same time taught to share in his virtues and sufferings, so that we may also live and reign eternally together with him."[9] In the Holy Eucharist the faithful find the experience of the resurrection. After Holy Communion, the clergy pronounce, "We have seen the resurrection of Christ," which the whole ecclesial congregation also declares on the Sundays after the morning resurrection Gospel. As Saint Symeon the New Theologian notes, the divine saying is not, "We have believed the resurrection of Christ," but "We have seen the resurrection of Christ . . . that is, that the resurrection of Christ occurs in each of us, the faithful."[10] Thus, the faithful share in the life of the resurrection, not only after, but also before their physical death.

The Christian as a member of the body of Christ and sharing in his cross and resurrection is received into communion with the Triadic God. The possibility which has been offered to man by the incarnation of God the Word — "he gave them the power to become children of God" (Jn 1.12) — is experienced personally. The Christian acquires this authority to call God "Father" by the grace of God and by his own co-operation. And so the ethical sense which the truth of adoption in Christ contains is revealed. Saint Gregory of Nyssa in one of his sermons *On the Lord's Prayer*, observes:

> But by calling him who is immortal, just and good "Our Father," [Christ teaches us] to demonstrate our family rights in our lives. Do you see how much preparation is needed? What kind of life? How much and what kind of care there must be so that at some time, when our conscience has been raised to this measure of freedom, we might dare to say to God, "Our Father?"

The uniqueness of a Christian as a child of God requires an analogous manner of life. No one is justified in calling God, "Father," if he is not concerned to confirm this kinship with his life as well. "When we approach God, then, first let us examine our life, to see if we have within us anything worthy of this divine kinship."[12] To invoke God as "Father" cannot be conventional. Christ who prompts the faithful to invoke God as "Father" does not permit lies. Adoption in Christ creates the ethical demand for a general relationship of the faithful with God the Father. To neglect this ethical dimension changes Christian theology into an ideology.

The Christian life exists in the final analysis as a participation in the kingdom of God which has been revealed and is active in the world, the Church. The nature of the Christian life is eschatological, as is the nature of the Church to which the faithful belong. Separation from this perspective entails its total alienation. And the restriction of the Christian proclamation to an intra-mundane framework constitutes a blatant forgery of it.

The Church is not a worldly organism that it can be defined in time and place and judged on the basis of its offering in history. The limitation of the Church to wordliness would mean the falsification of its identity. The Church transcends time and unites the past and the future to its present. The Church offers man the victory against time, the transcendance of death and participation in the eternal life of God.[13] Here also is found the characteristic mark of the Church: If the Church loses this distinctive quality, it has no reson to exist. If it is simply maintained as an establishment of use only to social and political life, it can best be forgotten in our revolutionary age and something new be sought in its place. Only if it transcends time and death and gives an eternal meaning to our life, can the Church maintain its indispensable place and mission.

Recent theology has the tendency to limit the proclamation to life on earth, to make faith easier for man. At the same time, it sets aside the central themes of forgiveness of sins, the victory against death and participation in eternal life in Christ. But in this way, the Christian proclamation is destroyed and the Christian life is made miserable: "If we have hoped in Christ in this life only, we are the most to be pitied of all" (1 Cor 15.19). In this case, men are justifiably led to decide to withdraw from the Church.

In order for the Church to protect her members from error, it has defined dogmas. The appearance of heresies was the ground for the formulation of dogmas. The characteristic mark of all heresies which the Church has condemned lies in that they dispute in whole or in part the truth of man's renewal and deification in Christ. By its dogmas, the Church has marked out the boundaries (*synora*) in relation to the deviations which have appeared at different times, and therefore, the Church's dogmas are called "definitions" (*oroi*).

The dogmas neither exhaust nor patrify the Church's truth. They express her living experience, that Jesus is the Christ in whose person has been realized the communion of God with man. The synoptic presentation of the dogmatic teaching of the Church is characterized, as is well konwn, as a "Symbol" of faith. In this way, the symbolic character of dogma is indicated. Besides, at the time that the ecclesial dogmas were formulated, the apophatic theology was being developed which leads beyond any positive or negative theological formulation.

Considering the Church's dogma from the view-point of Christian ethics, we can note the following points.

The dogma of the Trinity presents Christian love in its absolute form. Each person of the Holy Trinity is perfect God. The persons of the Divinity are not distinguished by the possession of essence, but according to the difference of their hypostatic properties. The Father is unbegotten, the Son begotten, the Spirit proceeds. The mutual love of the three persons does not exist as a movement toward selfish receiving, but as an expression of unity and completeness. The Triadic God is love, and the dogma of the Triadic God is the proclamation of divine love.

The Church replied to the controversy over the divinity of Chist which was undertaken by Arius with the dogma that the Son is perfect God, consubstantial with the Father. This dogma belongs to the study of the Trinity, but constitutes at the same time the foundation of christology.

Christ is not a man who was made God, but God who was made man. The deification of human nature was not a moral accomplishment, but a divine gift. Whatever man may do, he cannot transcend his createdness. He does not have by nature "a capacity to attain deification."[14] If Christ was not God by nature, but a creature, he could not save man. Then the Church's experience of man's renewal and deification would fall into the void. But as God who became man, Christ opened to man the way of deification. The moral renewal of man does not constitute the means but the fruit of salvation and renewal in Christ. God saves and renews man. Man co-operates in the work of his salvation and renewal. Thus, the teaching of Arius was not a dogmatic heresy, which opposed the man become God to the person of the Word of God made man, but also a moral heresy which opposed man's moral deification to his deification by grace.

In pre-Nicene theology, the Son of God is considered chiefly on the plane of the divine economy. He is the pre-existent Word of God, the Angel (Messenger) of his great counsel, who reveals his power and salvific activity. Therefore, he is called not only Son, but also Word and power and wisdom of God.[15]

The eternity of the Son of God is posited with the declaration of the consubstantiality of the Son with the Father. The Son and the Word of God is the second person of the consubstantial and undivided Trinity. It is characteristic that immediately after the formulation of the "consubstantiality" and parallel to the formulation of the christological dogma, the teaching about the distinction between the essence and energies of God was developed. This position which expresses the empirical character of the revelation of God, was included in Christian theology from the beginning, but it was stressed especially by the great Fathers of the fourth and fifth centuries.

Christ as perfect God and perfect man possesses "the whole fulness of deity bodily" (Col 2.9), and "we have all received from his fulness, grace for grace" (Jn 1.16). The grace of God which is a divine evergy creates the new man in Christ. Whatever happens to Christ, happens for man. Whatever his human nature acquires from the divinity, he transmits to Christians who are members of his body. Also so christology is simultaneously anthropology.

Christological dogma presents the "definitions" which insure the truth of the new life which is offered in Christ to man. This can be felt in the whole course of the formulation of the christological dogma. The positions of the Church against Apollinarianism, Nestorianism, Monophysitism, and Monothelitism, constitute special confirmations of this truth.

Apollinarianism questioned the fulness of the salvation of man in Christ. According to this teaching, the Son of God assumed human nature without a reasonable soul. The Church opposed this view saying that Christ assumed the whole human nature. If Christ had not assumed the whole human nature, man's salvation would not be complete: "For what is not assumed is not united to God is not saved.[16]

Nestorianism rejected the real union of the divine with the human nature in Christ. Thus it divided Christ into two persons, one divine and one human. According to Nestorios, the Blessed Virgin gave birth to the man Christ who is not personally united with the Son of God. Therefore according to the Nestorians, the Blessed Virgin cannot be called Mother of God but only Mother of Christ. But in this way, the salvation and renewal of man is rendered invalid. The mystery of his deification is abandoned.

The Blessed Virgin, who became the container of the Uncontained God and Mother of the Unbegotten, sums up the whole mystery of the economy in Christ in her person, The Blessed Virgin receives the unapproachable God and forms him as man. And this event is the mystery into which every person is initiated in the Church. Each of the faithful accepts and forms Christ within himself. And so each of the faithful takes the place of the Blessed Virgin and offers himself in order that Christ be formed within him, "My children, with whom I am again in labor until Christ be formed in you" (Gal 4.19). Like the Blessed Virgin, every Christian receives God and becomes a mother of God. Therefore, to deny the characterization of the Blessed Virgin as Mother of God (Theotokos) is to deny the mystery of the incarnation of God and the deification of man.

Monophysitism dissolves the human nature of Christ. By the Church's position against this heresy, it confirms that man's salvation is not realized by his absorption and disappearance in the divine nature. In Christ, the divine nature is united to human nature "without confusion, without change, without division, without separation."[17] Thus everyone who is united to God remains truly human while sharing in the divine grace.

Finally, the formulation of the christological dogma in opposition to monothelitism constitutes finally a pointer to ethical life. With its position in opposition to this heresy, the Church sets forth the importance of that human co-operation which is realized by the submission of the human will to the divine will. As it is with Christ, so each of the faithful is called to submit his will to the will of God.

When man offers his entire will to God, he takes everything from God. God needs nothing from man; God is self-sufficient. Whatever

happens to or is revealed by Christ, happens and is revealed for man.
Christ's victory over death, his resurrection and ascension to the glory
of the Father, is a victory for man over death; it is his own resurrection and assumption to the glory of God. The truth of man and his
life is defined by the struggle against the christological heresies. And
a struggle is noted where the truth is contested that Jesus is the Christ
in whose person the renewal and deification of man is realized.
Christology defines the anthropology of the new man. Every
counterfeit of christology is simultaneously a counterfeit of the
Church's anthropology. When new anthropological elements in the
area of theology are taken up, there are corresponding repercussions
in christology. This is happening in contemporary theology. Thus the
attempt of modern theologians to introduce modern anthropology
into theology is combined with a disorientation of christology, in the
framework of which the so-called christology "from below" (*von unten*)
has appeared.[18] But it must be noted that a pure christology "from
below" constitutes in reality a new form of the adoptionism which
was condemned by the Church.

The truth of the Church is the truth of Christ. This truth does
not lose its timeliness for man and his life. Even the secularization
of our time has left untouched the area to which it refers.[19] But the
revelation of this truth requires at every time the language of its era,
just as the disputes over it occur each time in the language of that
era. The Church, living the truth of Christ, distinguishes the transfor-
mations which the disputes over this truth have assumed in each age
and the kinship which these disputes display amongst them. Thus
on the same basis, it can establish its position in every age, just as
its opposition does in each new challenge.

The theology of the Church, like the Church itself, has needed
an organic development in the course of history, it cannot fulfil its
goal fixed in a static condition. But in modern theology, a persistent
tendency for modernism has appeared which is something different
from organic development. In modernism, there is always the danger
of continuity being broken. In an organic development of theology,
a creative repetition is assumed of what already exists. This is confirmed in patristic theology. Saint John of Damascus in his work, *The*

Fount of Knowledge, writes:

> I will say nothing, as I have said, of my own. When I have gathered
> he labors of the most eminent teachers into one, so far as I am able,
> I will make an abridgement of the text, being obedient in everything
> to your command.[20]

This does not mean that Saint John of Damascus merely copied
the earlier Fathers, but that he composed his work supporting and
expressing the common tradition. Just as the birth of each man is
a repetition at the same time that it is a new creation, so also a living
theology is a repetition and a new creation.

The maintenance of the Church's unity contributes to the
maintenance of the unity of theology, while the preservation of the
unity of theology confirms the preservation of the unity of the Church.
Heresy is found on the opposite side. It constitutes a constant threat
to the maintenance of the Church's unity and theology. Continually
threatening the Church's identity and theology, it forms disunity. It
is characteristic that even after the period of the christological heresies,
the Church saw in the heresies which appeared the revival of the old
christological heresies. Thus, in the teaching of the iconoclasts, it
discerned the revival of Arianism, Nestorianism, or Monophysitism
in a new form or expression.

The iconoclasts were not combating only the images of Christ,
but the honor of the saints as well, their relics and their icons. They
denied the real presence of God in the world and the transmission
of the grace of God by means of matter. They made matter autonomous and rejected the possibility of its transformation. They con-
verted theology into an ideology. On the pretext that they were fighting
idolatrous and magical understandings, they secularized the Church
and divided the world from God and his grace. Thus, the iconoclasts
invalidated the immanence of God in the world, which is founded
on the incarnation and maintained in the Holy Eucharist, in the bread
and wine which are changed into body and blood of Christ.

The Church does not disdain matter because even this was created
by God. Matter is not independent of God, but the sensible presence

of the divine will: "None of the things that are was fashioned from some underlying matter into what is apparent, but the divine will became matter and essence of the things that were created.[21] God himself became matter and dwells in matter and accomplishes man's salvation by means of matter. Therefore, the Christian honors matter, not as God of course, "but as filled with divine activity and grace."[22]

Later, when the truth of man's renewal and deification in Christ was not contested any longer by direct reference to the person of Christ or to the possibility of his representation, but on the level of mystical experience, the ecclesial teaching was supported by the use of the distinction between essence and energy in God. God's essence remains inaccessible and imparticipable, while his energies become accessible and participable.[23] This teaching, as we have said, is stressed especially in the theology of the fourth and fifth centuries. During the fourteenth century, we have the organic development of this same teaching. Thus, we come to the teaching of Saint Gregory Palamas about the uncreated energies of God. The uncreated energies of God are distinguished from his uncreated essence. Without this distinction, one is led either into pantheism or to the denial of real communion between God and the world, in which case all the previous dogmas of the Church are unsupported and groundless. Therefore, it is not accidental that Saint Gregory Palamas saw in the persons of the enemies of the hesychastic teaching a distillation of the previous heresies. The question is proposed again, that is, of the communion of man with God and of deification. The positions of Saint Gregory Palamas supported this communion and deification while the understandings of his opponents rejected them. They denied the uncreated energies of God producing the most ancient heresies again in a new form.

The theology of the uncreated energies assumes the entire tradition of the Orthodox Church. It assumes among other things, prayer, discipline, obedience, fasting, humility, liturgical life, and eucharistic communion. It is the same patristic theology in a new language. This theology in a new age could be offered only in a new language. This is living theology. Herein lies the functionality or the disfunctionality of theology. When there is a living bearer, it can function. When this bearer does not exist, theology is led either into modernism or is frozen in conservatism.

Saint Basil the Great
On the Holy Spirit[24]

God our Savior planned to recall man from the fall. Man's disobedience separated him from God's household, and God wished to bring him back. This is why Christ took flesh, and accomplished everything described in the Gospels: his sufferings, the cross, the tomb, the resurrection, so that man might be saved through imitation of Christ and receive his original birthright. If we are to be perfect we must not only imitate Christ's meekness, humility, and long-suffering, but his death as well. Paul surely was an imitator of Christ, and he says, "that I may know him and the power of his resurrection, and may share his sufferings, becoming like him in his death, that is possible I may attain the resurrection from the dead" (Phil 3.10-11).

How can we become like him in his death? By being buried with him in baptism (Rom 6.4). What kind of burial is it, and what is gained from such imitation?

First, it is necessary that the old way of life be terminated, and this is impossible unless a man is born again, as the Lord has said (Jn 3.3). Regeneration, as its very name reveals, is a beginning of a second life. Before beginning a second life, one must put an end to the first. When a runner has to run around the post at the end of the racetrack in order to return on the other side of the course, he has to stop and pause momentarily, in order to negotiate such a sharp turn. So also if we are going to change our lives, death must come between what has already happened (ending it) and what is just beginning.

How can we accomplish this descent into death? By imitating the burial of Christ through baptism. The bodies of those being baptized are buried in the water. Thus baptism signifies the putting off of the works of the flesh, as the Apostle says: "In him also you were circumcised with a circumcision made without hands, by putting off the body of flesh in the circumcision of Christ; and you were buried with him in baptism" (Col 2.11-12). The filth which has grown on the soul by the working of a carnal mind is washed away. "Wash me, and I shall be whiter than snow" (Ps 51.7). In this respect we differ from the Jews: they wash themselves after each defilement, but we know that the baptism of salvation is received only once, since he died for the world once, and rose from the dead once, and baptism is a figure of his death and resurrection.

The Lord who gives us life also gave us the baptismal covenant, which contains an image of both death and life. The image of death is fulfilled in the water, and the Spirit gives us the pledge of life. Therefore it is clear why water is associated with the Spirit: because of baptism's dual purpose. On the one hand, the body of sin is destroyed, that it may never bear fruit for death. On the other hand, we are made to live by the Spirit, and bear fruit in holiness. The water receives our body as a tomb, and so becomes the image of death, while the Spirit pours in life-giving power, renewing in souls which were dead in sin the life they first possessed. This is what it means to be born again of water and Spirit: the water accomplishes our death, while the Spirit raises us to life. This great sign of baptism is fulfilled in three immersions, with three invocations, so that the image of death might be completely formed, and the newly-baptized might have their souls enlightened with divine knowledge. If there is any grace in the water, it does not come from the nature of the water, but from the Spirit's presence, since baptism is not a removal of dirt from the body, but an appeal to God for a clear conscience (1 Pt 3.21).

The Lord describes in the Gospel the pattern of life we must be trained to follow after the (baptismal) resurrection: gentleness, endurance, freedom from the defiling love of pleasure, and from covetousness. We must be determined to acquire in this life all the qualities of the life to come. To define the Gospel as a description of what resurrectional life should be like seems to be correct and appropriate, as far as I am concerned.

NOTES

[1] *The Hagioritic Tome*, "Prologue," in Saint Gregory Palamas, *Erga* 3, 496.

[2] *On the Holy Spirit* 12, PG 32.116B.

[3] Saint Epiphanios of Cyprus, *Against Heresies*, 69.65, PG 42.309A.

[4] Theodore Kyros, *Interpretation of the Song of Songs*, 3.6, PG 81.120.

[5] Saint Nicholas Kabasilas, *The Life in Christ*, 2.6, p. 75.

[6] Origen, *Commentary on John* 10.20, PG 19.372B, cf. Rom 6.3-5.

[7] *The Life in Christ* 1.6, p. 49-50.

[8] Ibid. 4.1, p. 113. of Saint Symeon of Thessalonike, *On the Sacred Ceremonies*, 68, PG 155.233B.

[9] Saint Gregory Palamas, *Homily* 56.16, *Erga* 11,418.

[10] *Discourses* 13.4 B. Krivocheine (ed), Sources Chretiénnes, 104 (Paris, 1964), p. 198.

[11] *On the Lord's Prayer* 2.3.

[12] Ibid. 2.5.

[13] The past and the future are present in the Church here and now. And the man who exists here and now lives in eternity.

[14] Saint Maximos Confessor, *Various Texts* 1.75, *Philokalia* 2, 181; PG 90.1209C.

[15] e.g. v. Jn 1.1; Justin Martyr, *First Apology*, 33, PG 6.381B; Clement of Alexandria, *Miscellanies* 7.2, PG 9.412B.

[16] Saint Gregory the Theologian, *Letter* 101 "To Kledonios," PG 37.181C-4A.

[17] Council of Chalcedon, *Definition*, ET in Edward R. Hardy, *Christology of the Later Fathers* (Philadelphia, 1954), pp. 372-4.

[18] See further A. Schilson, W. Kasper, *Christologie im Präsens*, Freiburg, 1980, p. 115ff; W. Kasper, *Jesus the Christ*, tr. V. Green (London & New York, 1976), p. 247.

[19] cf. H. Lübbe, *Religion nach der Aufklärung* (Graz, 1986), p. 178.

[20] PG 94.525A and cf. 533A. Leontios of Byzantium, *Against Nestorios and Eutyches*, PG 86.1344D.

[21] Saint Gregory of Nyssa, *Homily on 1st Corinthians*, 15.28 PG 44.1312A.

[22] Saint John of Damascus, *On the Divine Image*, 1, PG 94.1300AB.

[23] "Imparticipable" and "participable" refer to the impossibility and possibility, respectively, of participating or sharing in the divine nature and energies and were coined to translate characteristic terms in the theology of Saint Gregory Palamas. See further G.I. Mantzaridis, *The Deification of Man*, tr. Liadain Sherrard (Crestwood, 1984), p. 104 ff.-tr.

[24] Tr. David Anderson (Crestwood, 1980), pp. 57-59. Paragraph divisions have been added.

Love your neighbor as yourself
— Passion keeps you from stepping out of yourself and "being" your neighbor

God uses the sickness as our cure—forces us to go to others, i.e. community

CHAPTER SEVEN

The Divine Liturgy and the World

"My father is working still, and I am working" (Jn 5.17). The work of God the Father and of Christ for the world is that work which is realized for the perfection of the world. Moreover, the perfection of the world, which is God's creation, presupposes the world's participation in God's work. The world's creation, presupposes the world's participation in the work which God realizes for it constitutes its ministry (λειτουργία). By participating in God's work the world ministers and is liturgized. This ministry of the world is carried out with one aim in view; it is done with the perspective that God offers to the world, and that is the world's perfection.

Without the perspective which God offers to the world, any movement or direction the world takes is essentially purposeless. The world's life itself is purposeless, because it cannot have any meaning whatsoever. Its life becomes a sort of death that can only serve death. Moreover, the people living this life are not actually living, but are the walking dead; they are the dead that bury "their own dead" (Mt 8.22).

On the phenomenal level, life appears as movement which is manifested either as energy or as passion. It is expressed as energy when it affirms human nature, and as passion when it denies or surpasses human nature. Saint Maximos the Confessor notes the following:

> That of effecting is one principle, and that of experiencing is another. On the one hand, the principle of effecting is the natural power to accomplish virtues. On the other hand, the principle of experiencing is either the acceptance of the grace for that which is beyond nature or the agreement with that which is contrary to nature. For as we do not have the natural power for the beyond-being, thus neither do we have the power by nature for the non-being. Therefore we experience as being beyond nature by grace, but we cannot effect deification for we do not have by nature the power capable of it. Again, we experience as being against nature by the agreement of our free will with evil, for we do not have the natural power to do evil. Therefore, while we are here, we perform virtues by nature since we have the natural power to do so.[1]

From the viewpoint of the natural sciences, man is the most unnatural thing in nature. The most natural things are the elements of nature. Man becomes more natural when he is disintegrated into the natural elements that compose him, in other words when he dies.

Yet man is not a mere natural being, but the ecstatic being in the world. An ecstatic being means one that surpasses itself and is turned toward something outside of itself. In theological language, man's ecstatic nature is indicated by his distinction as a creature "according to the image and likeness of God." An image does not have meaning except in relation to that which reflects. Moreover, likeness is incomprehensible without reverence to a prototype. Consequently, man as a creature "according to the image and likeness of God" cannot be understood independently of God. With this presupposition, man's relation to God comprises his "natural" condition. Moreover, the lack of this relationship is not merely a moral omission, but a basic ontological fall, just as Saint Gregory of Nyssa notes: "For nothing would remain in existence if it did not remain in the being. Moreover, the foremost and primary being is the divine being. The fact that all things remain in existence compels us to believe that this divine being exists in them."[2] Thus, man's preservation within the state of being is not a static event, but rather a dynamic one which is realized as his transcendence over continually threatening annihilation. This transcendence is not understood except in relation to the being, namely God, that can preserve man in a state of existence. Therefore, man's relation to God is his ontological need and indispensable presupposition for the preservation of his "natural" condition.

The life of virtue corresponds to man's natural condition. As Saint Maximos the Confessor observes: "Therefore, while we are here, we perform virtues by nature, since we have the natural power to do so." Just as man's natural condition has an ecstatic character, so, too, does his natural life, the life of virtue, have an ecstatic character; that is, it surpasses man and is turned outside of him. This means that the worth of man or of his life cannot be realized within the bounds of his natural energy but far beyond them.

Indeed, man cannot stay within the bounds of his natural virtue, and for this reason he is unavoidably led to passion. Passion responds to man's ecstatic character exactly because it carries him outside himself. This means that passion also responds to man's natural life, to the life of virtue, for it too has an ecstatic character. Thus, the full realization of man and of his virtues is found unavoidably in passion.

Passion though, as Saint Maximos comments, appears either as "the acceptance of the grace for that which is beyond nature" or as "the agreement with that which is contrary to nature." The "supernatural grace," or "supernatural passion," which also gives value to the realization of man's natural being, keeps man within the perspective of his ontological existence as an image of God. On the contrary, agreement with that which is contrary to nature or "unnatural" passion diverts man from his ontological perspective and alienates him. Supernatural passion is unlimited perfection, whereas unnatural passion is the fall into non-existence. "Supernatural passion is unlimited since it is active, while unnatural passion is inactive."[3]

Whatever is applicable for man is valid for the world in its totality. The whole world has its cause and relation in the Logos of God, "for in him were all things created" (Col 1.16). As an image of the Logos of God to whom the principles (λόγοι) of all things refer back, man recapitulates the principles of all things according to the image of God the Logos. For this reason, in patristic writings, man is characterized as a microcosm and link of all creation.[4]

Thus, man is the only means of relation between the world and God. Man is the priest of the world who is called to perform the cosmic liturgy. Yet when he himself does not do this but lives aimlessly, then the world is not oriented towards its purpose but moves aimlessly along with man; "the whole creation has been groaning in travail together until now" (Rom 8.22). Thus, the world's relation with God became impossible after man's fall. The world, deprived of man's supernatural passion, is not simply confined to the natural, but is unavoidably led to the unnatural.

Whatever is natural in the world is defined by time. The world exists and moves in time. Whatever occurs in the world takes place in time and is defined by time. Moreover, whatever man does or thinks, he does or thinks within time and under its definitive power. Time then defines the world without being defined by it. Simultaneously, though, time is interwoven with the world which it defines and is not understood independently of it. This means that time, which defines the world, is defined in turn by some other reality which is unaccessible to the world because it is beyond time. This reality is supernatural reality, the reality of God.

This supernatural reality is inaccessible and incomprehensible for the world because the world, which is unable to act or think independently of time, is incapable of knowing or understanding anything outside of itself whatsoever. This is why God, who is inaccessible and incomprehensible to the world, is revealed in time and finally becomes himself a man to be known by men. In this case time, which is lifted as a separating barrier between the natural and the supernatural, between the cosmic and the world — and specifically man who lives is time and cannot do anything without it — receives the revelation of the transcendental in time and participates in it by means of time.

God's work in the world is realized exclusively for the world. The very presence of God as a man within the world is made with the unique objective of the realization of man.

> The Lord, who is uncreated in his own divinity, became whatever he became for us. The life which he lived for us, showing us the way which leads us back to true life. Whatever he suffered in his flesh he suffered for us, healing our passions. On account of our sin, he was led to death and he rose and ascended for us, providing for us the resurrection and ascension forever.[5]

God's work for the world is summarized and continued in the Divine Liturgy. For this reason the importance of the Divine Liturgy for the world is primary. The essence of the Divine Liturgy is the Holy Eucharist, the remembrance of Christ. However, what is this remembrance of Christ and how is it made?

Nicholas Kabasilas notes that the remembrance of Christ is not made with the remembrance of his powerful deeds, but with the remembrance of his weakness and death. Thus, for his remembrance he did not ask us to recall that he resurrected the dead, gave sight to the blind, rebuked the winds, etc. "Rather we must remember those events which seem to denote nothing but weakness: his cross, his passion, his death — these are the happenings which he asks us to commemorate."[6]

Saint Paul addressing the Christians of Corinth wrote the following:

> For I received from the Lord what I also delivered to you, that the Lord Jesus on the night when he was betrayed took bread, and when he had given thanks, he broke it, and said, 'This is my body which is broken for you. Do this in remembrance of me.' In the same way also the cup, after supper, saying, 'This cup is the new covenant in my blood. Do this, as often as you drink it, in remembrance of me' (1 Cor 11.23-25).

However, the remembrance of the passion and death of Christ, as a remembrance of the same Christ who arose, is always made within the light of his resurrection. It is characteristic that the day *par excellence* of this remembrance, the day of the Holy Eucharist, is not Friday but Sunday. Furthermore, it should be noted that on the day of Christ's passion, Great and Holy Friday, the Orthodox Church does not allow the celebration of the Divine Liturgy. The Divine Liturgy is the remembrance of Christ's passion and death which only has meaning, in the light of his resurrection.

The remembrance of Christ, the Holy Eucharist, essentially summarizes the tradition of the Church. His tradition, as revealed in the very Eucharist does not aim to preserve the remembrance of one event in time, but to transfigure time and the world which exists in time, uniting time with its truth. As that supper by which the many become "one body" (1 Cor 10.17), the Holy Eucharist puts against time an intertimely reality, the Church which has its foundation in the person of Christ. In this way the Church initiates man's, and with him the whole world's, relation to God. Thus, whatever the first Adam and his descendents did not accomplish, the new Adam, Christ — and in Christ the whole eucharistic body, the Church — does, accomplish. In the Eucharist, therefore, the Church serves as the priest of the world and offers the world of God.[7]

This new reality that is revealed in the Church surpasses the definitive power of time and functions in the world as an expression of God's presence. The Church's body, which is the very body of Christ, reveals the mystery of the triadic communion in the world and encompasses man within it. Just as each person of the Holy Trinity exists integrally by itself, each also exists wholly in each of the other person of the Trinity, and furthermore exists wholly in the totality of the triadic communion. Thus, Christ — and similarly the Trinitarian God — exists totally in himself, exists wholly in every believer, and also exists wholly in the total communion of the faithful, in the Church.[8]

Usually, we identify the resurrected body of Christ with the body which his disciples saw during his various appearances from the resurrection to the ascension, and we forget that the resurrected body of Christ is also the Church, the Church not as an established institution, but as a eucharistic communion, a communion of deification. Christ was not resurrected for himself but for the world. Moreover, the resurrected Christ is not only the person of the resurrected Logos of God, who in fact was never found under death's authority; he is also the Church.[9]

The Church is extended into the world by means of the Holy Eucharist. Each of the faithful who participates in the Holy Eucharist is united with the body of Christ to which all the other faithful of the Church also belong — not only the living, but also those who lived in the past and those who will live in the future. The body of Christ surpasses time and space and joins all its members in the triadic communion where all things are present and live in the Lord. Within the body of Christ, namely in the Church, there is neither lost time nor lost people. Whatever God did in the past for the salvation of the world exists always as present and can be made accessible to each person. For this reason, every year, and in fact every day of the year, the Church succinctly presents the whole mystery of God's work for the salvation of the world. Thus, within the yearly cycle of feasts, the Church celebrates the Annunciation of the Theotokos, the Nativity of Christ, his baptism, his teaching and ministry, the Transfiguration, the cross, the burial, the Resurrection, the Ascension, and finally Pentecost.

Each one of these feast days is not a mere remembrance, but a liturgical repetition of that day on which the celebrated event actually took place. In this way, for example, the feast day of the Annunciation repeats liturgically the revelation of "the hidden mystery of the ages"; "Today [is] the beginning of our salvation and the revelation of the mystery of the ages." The same also holds true for the feast days of the Nativity of the Crucifixion of Christ. Each of these feasts is not a mere remembrance but a liturgical repetition of the corresponding even which was actualized within human history. "Today Christ is born of a virgin in Bethlehem" or "Today he who hung the earth on waters is hung on a cross." Thus, within the framework of each separate day, the Church lives and presents the fundamental events of divine economy. Thus, for example, at the third hour we are carried liturgically to the descent of the Holy Spirit, at the sixth hour to the crucifixion, and at the ninth hour to Christ's death.

Distance of time and place are annihilated, and all things become present in Christ. Just as Christ as the Lord of glory is beyond time and place, so too whatever belongs to his body or whatever relates to it also surpasses time and place and is preserved eternally present. This is why Christians who abandon this world are not considered dead by "asleep." They are not lost in the oblivion of time, but remain immortal in the Church's memory. The Theotokos, John the Forerunner, the apostles, the prophets, the righteous, the saints, and all those who have fallen asleep in the Lord in the Church triumphant, which comprises the organic continuation of the militant Church in which we live today.

This truth is expressed in an incomparable way in the very chalice of the Holy Eucharist. As we all know, not only is the "Lamb," namely the body of Christ, placed in the chalice, but finally also the portions for the Theotokos, the apostles, and all the saints. In this way, the faithful, participating in the holy cup, participate in the whole body of the Church which as Christ as its head and all those, living or asleep, who believe in him as its members.

Exactly for this reason is Holy Communion of essential importance for the life of the world. It is the signpost for the world's life which does not lead it only as far as death, but which gives it worth even beyond death. As it was correctly noted: "Life which lacks the infinite, unlimited dimensions of death is lifelessness and death itself. This is why life which is as powerful as death has as its gate the death of everything corruptible."[10]

The Holy Eucharist, as we all know, is not a mystery which is repeated, but a mystery which is celebrated continually "for the life of the world." It is not actualized outside the world, nor does it take place along the margin of the world. The Holy Eucharist takes place at the heart of the world, and without it the world cannot truly live.

The Eucharist is essentially completed in Christ, and thus it can be celebrated continually. God "who is rich in mercy, out of the great love with which he loved us . . . made us alive together with Christ . . . and raised us up with him, and made us sit with him in the heavenly places in Christ Jesus" (Eph 2.4-6).

The world is not called to realize the Holy Eucharist, but to participate in it. The Holy Eucharist is the liturgy in which the world is invited to participate. It is invited to participate because otherwise it will not be able to function. Everything which exists, in the world finds its place in the Divine Liturgy and it is liturgized. Along with the world, the history of the world is also liturgized because Christ is also the Lord of history. But in order to bring something to the liturgy, it is imperative that it be baptized; in other words, that it die on the phenomenal level. Here lies the great challenge for the world.

People that are far from God think they are secure only on the phenomenal level. Thus, they refuse to become transparent and to find themselves again on a higher plane. For Christianity though "good does not reside in what our eyes can see; the fact that Jesus Christ is now within the Father is why we perceive him so much the more clearly."[11] The truth for the world and man is found beyond the deceptiveness of phenomena. For this reason, all that is wordly or human finds its value only as a symbol of the eucharistic reference to God.

The whole Divine Liturgy has a symbolic character. Nicholas Kabasilas in his *Commentary on the Divine Liturgy* observes:

> Not only the chants and readings but the very actions themselves have this part to play; each has its own immediate purpose and usefulness. But at the same time each symbolizes some part of the works of Christ, his deeds or his sufferings. For example, we have the bringing of the Gospel to the altar, then the bringing of the offerings. Each is done for a purpose, the one that the Gospel may be read, the other that the sacrifice may be performed; besides this, however, one represents the appearance and the other the manifestation of the Savior; the first, obscure and imperfect, at the beginning of his life; the second, the perfect and supreme manifestation.[12]

The Divine Liturgy, unravels itself symbolically and offers itself by means of perceptible symbols. Man participates in the liturgy with these perceptible symbols of the Divine Liturgy. In the Divine Liturgy the whole world is wholely recapitulated. So the whole world also becomes simultaneously a symbol. Man, who participates in the liturgy, discovers in its perceptible symbols the world's true symbolic meaning.

When the perceptible also ceases to be symbols, then the liturgy stops being divine.

Today, we are undergoing the problem of man's participation in the Divine Liturgy. What is usually suggested as a panacea for the solution of this problem is the translation of the Divine Liturgy into the vernacular of the faithful. The language of the Divine Liturgy, so it is said, is usually not comprehensible to the average believer of our times. To help him participate in the liturgy, we must translate the Divine Liturgy into his language.

However, the language consists of a partial area within the very wide symbolic system of the Divine Liturgy. Thus, for example, aside from the language, we have various liturgical acts, the way of delivering the readings, the music, painting, and architecture. All these comprise the language of the Divine Liturgy in the wider sense of the world. This is why an attempt that aims at making the Divine Liturgy comprehensible to today's man cannot be limited to the translation of its texts, but must also be extended to the translation of all the other symbolic means with which the Divine Liturgy is associated and which comprise its language in the wider sense of the word.

However, all of the symbols or expressive means of the Divine Liturgy which were formulated over a prolonged period of natural development corresponding to the spiritual development of their bearers, are received by us as established objectifications. These objectifications simultaneously comprise means, but also obstacles for our participation in church. They are means of our participation because they were created and used for the same goal. They are also obstacles precisely because they are offered as objectifications of the spiritual life of generations that lived in times and conditions which are very distant from us.

Therefore, the problem of the contemporary world's participation in the Divine Liturgy is a widespread and complicated one that demands a catholic and many-faceted confrontation. For us to participate correctly in the liturgy today, a liturgy in our language is not enough. Even more so, a translation of the traditional liturgy into today's language does not suffice because in this case, aside from its inadequacy, the illusion of the proper churches, the proper icons, the proper texts, the proper music, the proper expressive symbols, we must start from nothing, at which we have just arrived. To begin properly, we need to begin seeing the world symbolically once again. In this perspective, the whole world becomes a symbol of the personal relationship of God with man and of man with God. Within the bounds of this symbolic relation, man and the world find their realization.

Saint Cyril of Alexandria
On the Gospel of John 11.11

Therefore there is, as it were, a beginning and way for us to get a share of the Holy Spirit (Heb 6.4).

The mystery of our union with God was established on Christ; for we are all sanctified in him, in the manner already said. The Only Begotten contrived a way, discovered through the wisdom proper to himself and through the council of the Father, so that we might enter into unity with God and with one another and that we ourselves may be associated together (although separated into an individuality both of body and soul by the perceived difference of each one). For by one body, his own, that is, he blesses those who believe in him and he makes them to be of one body with himself and with one another through the mystical communion.

For who would divine and remove the natural union between each of them who through one holy body are bound into unity in Christ? For if we all share in the one bread, we all are one body (cf. 1 Cor 10.17). For it is not possible that Christ be divided (cf. 1 Cor 1.13). Therefore, the Church bears the title "Body of Christ," and we are all individually members of it, according to the understanding of Paul (Eph 5.30). For we are all united to Christ through his holy body, seeing that we have all received the one and indivisible [body] into our own bodies. Surely, therefore, we owe our own members to him rather than to ourselves.

With the Savior appointed as the head, the Church, is then, called the "body," joined together as from individual members. Paul proves this when he says, " . . . so that we no longer be infants, tossed by the waves and carried about by every wind of men's deceitful teaching, of error's artful trickery. But speaking the truth in love, let us increase in all things in him who is the head, Christ. From him the whole body is fit together and held together through every supporting ligament and he causes the body to grow in accord with the strength appropriate to each part to build it up in love" (Eph 4.14-16).

I say, then, that we who have become participants of his holy body enjoy the perceived union with Christ according to the body. Again Paul testifies concerning the mystery of our religion when he says, "What was not known to the sons of men in other generations has now been revealed in the Spirit to his holy apostles and prophets: the nations are coheirs and co-participants in the promise in Christ" (Eph 3.5-6). If we are all of one body with one another in Christ, and not only with one another, but with him, that is, with him who is in us through his own body, how could we not clearly be one both in one another and in Christ already? For Christ is the bond of unity, being both God and man in himself.

NOTES

[1] Saint Maximos Confessor, *Various Chapters* 1.78; pg. 90, 1212 E.

[2] Saint Gregory of Nyssa, *Catechetical Oration* 32, ed. Srawley, p. 119; see ET in Edward R. Hardy (ed.), *Christology of the Later Fathers* (Philadelphia, 1954), p. 311.

[3] Saint Maximos Confessor, *Various Chapters* 1.77, PG 90.1212B; see *Philokalia*, 2, 182.

[4] See Methodios of Olympos, *On the Resurrection* 2.10; Saint Gregory the Theologian, *Sermon* 38.11, PG 36.324A; Kosmas Indikopleustes, *Christian Topography 5*, PG 88.230A.

[5] Saint Gregory Palamas, *Homily* 21.4, *Erga* 10,26.

[6] *A Commentary on the Divine Liturgy*, tr. J. M. Hussey and P. A. McNulty (New York, 1977), p. 36.

[7] See J. Zizioulas, "L' Eucharistie: Quelques aspects bibliques," *L' Eucharistie*, "Églises en dialogue" 12 (Mame, 1970), p. 65.

[8] See D. Staniloae, *The Mystagogy of Saint Maximos Confessor* (Athens, 1973), p. 209, note 65, in Greek.

[9] See also W. Pannenburg, "Die Auferstehung Jesu und die Zukunft des Menschen," in *Kerygma und Dogma* 24 (1978) 114 ff.

[10] See Archimandrite Vasilios, *Hymn of Entry*, tr. Elizabeth Briere (Crestwood,

1984), p. 69.

[11]Saint Ignatios of Antioch, *To the Romans* 3.3 in *Early Christian Writings* (New York, 1978), p. 104.

[12]*A Commentary on the Divine Liturgy*, pp. 27-28.

CHAPTER EIGHT

The Life of Worship

Worship is the center of the Church's life. All its other activities
— preaching, teaching, care, philanthropy — prepares or express its
worshipping life, and therefore remain indeterminate and insipid
without it. If worship is missing, the presence and work of the Church
have no meaning, while with worship at the centre, the presence and
work of the Church, as of each particular member, acquire sense and
purpose.

But what is worship and how is it born in the soul of man? Worship is the expression of love and devotion to God, which is born
from gratitude to him. When, for example, the man blind from birth
was healed by Christ, he felt a profound gratitude in his heart and
love for his benefactor, whom he still didn't know. When Christ later

appeared to him an asked him if he believed in him, he said, " 'I believe, Lord,' and worshipped him" (Jn 9.38). And so, the gratitude and love of the blind man who was healed were expressed with full devotion and worship. This "I believe, Lord" and his kneeling before Christ show, externally moreover, this faith in and worship of his benefactor.

The cause which led the man blind from birth to faith in and worship of Christ was the benefit that he received, that is, his healing. If there had not been the benefit, and also its recognition, to give birth to gratitude to the benefactor, there would not have been an expression of worship.

We see, then, that worship assumes two basic facts: the benefit and the recognition of the benefit. If these are missing, we do not really have worship. Transfering these facts to everyday religious life, we can say that, if there are religious expressions without connection to a parallel recognition of the benefit received from Christ, true worship is not realized. If the crosses or prostrations which are made, if the candles or the lamps which are lit do not express man's heartfelt gratitude for the benefits of Christ, they are not expressions of true worship.

But what are the benefits from Christ, whose recognition leads man to worship? The benefits of Christ to man after his creation and fall can be summarized as his salvation and renewal. The Apostle Paul writes:

> God, who is rich in mercy, because of his great love with which he loved us, has given life in Christ while we were dead in sins . . . and he has raised us and seated us in heavenly places in Christ Jesus (Eph 2.4-6).

Sin kills man. And since all men are born in sin and live in it, they are condemned to death. God, then, in his great love gives life to people condemned to death, and lifts them up to the throne of his glory as glorified members of the body of Christ, as his glorified children. It is enough to remember the well-known parable of the prodigal son. The rebellious son, since he had literally squandered all his portion of his father's property and brought his honor and reputation into disrepute, decided to return to his father and become his servant. But before he had time to return, his father ran and received him with great love, took him home like before and gave a splendid feast for his return, sacrificing "the fattened calf" (Lk 15.30).

This image of the father, who receives his rebellious but repentant child with love, helps us to feel somehow the love of God, who not only comes and meets each of his children who returns, but also sacrifices himself as "a fattened calf," in order to offer him salvation and life. When, then, man reflects on this offering of God, when he considers the greatness of his benefits, it is natural for him to feel that gratitude in his heart which constitutes the condition for true worship. Many times, certainly, man is ungrateful and does not feel the need to thank God for his benefits. Here, one can recall the ten lepers whom Christ healed. Only one of them, a Samaritan, returned to thank Christ. The remaining nine "did not return to give glory to God" (Lk 17.17).

The sense of God's benefits, which is the condition for real worship, also entails reconciliation with one's neighbor. No one can sense the wealth of God's love and grace before him and retain hatred and enmity to his neighbor. If this happens, it means that he does not respect the gift of God; it means, in other words, that he does not have the requisite conditions to worship God. Therefore, Christ in his Sermon on the Mount observes:

> If, then, you are offering your gift at the altar, and there you remember that your brother has something against you, leave your gift there before the altar, and first go to be reconciled with your brother. Then come and offer your gift (Mt 5.23-4).

In other words, God accepts man's gift only when he has love for his fellow men. If there is enmity and ill-will within him, no offering of his at all is acceptable to God.

Precisely for this reason, the first invitation which begins the supreme religious offering, the Divine Liturgy, is an invitation of peace: "In peace, let us pray to the Lord." This peace assumes reconciliation with our neighbor. When someone is at peace with his neighbor, then he can also be at peace with himself. This double peace, then, peace with our neighbor and peace with ourselves, constitutes the necessary condition for true worship of God.

All who are baptized in the name of Christ and participate in the mystery of the Holy Eucharist are members of his body. "We who are many," writes the Apostle Paul, "are one body in Christ, and members one of another" (Rom 12.5). This means that no one can be a Christian only for himself. From the moment that someone becomes a Christian, that is, from the moment that he is baptized, he is a part of a new body, the body of the Church, which has Christ himself as its head. Therefore, faith, prayer, worship and, in general, the whole life of the Christian is not simply his individual affair. The Christian cannot pray to God only for himself and be indifferent to his neighbor. On this point, the prayer which Christ himself gave as an example, the Lord's Prayer, is characteristic. In this prayer, God is addressed as the common Father of all the faithful: "Our Father in heaven." God is the Father of each of us, because he is the Father of Christ, to whose body we all belong.

The consequences of this truth are obvious. When we go to Church in order to worship God, we should not feel like isolated individuals who are fulfilling their religious obligations, but as brothers united in the name of Christ, as one undivided body with Christ as the head. This feeling was especially intense during the first centuries, when Christians were a minority in the world. But Christians should always have this feeling because otherwise they cannot be true Christians.

Worship, and especially the Divine Liturgy, is not a matter for the clergy, but of all the faithful. Of course, as we know, the Divine Liturgy in the Orthodox Church cannot be celebrated without a priest; but the priest cannot celebrate the Divine Liturgy by himself. The fulness of the Church is not just the clergy, but also the laity. The clergy preside at the divine worship as spiritual fathers of the laity. The laity are directed to God and receive his grace through the intermediary of the clergy. But all together, clergy and laity, are members of the one and undivided body of Christ, which is the Church.

The Divine liturgy begins with the recognition of God's love which reveals his kingdom on earth: "Blessed be the Kingdom of the Father and of the Son and of the Holy Spirit, now and forever and to the ages. Amen." A new world is opened to man: the true world, the kingdom of God, which transforms man and his life. Just as wine, when it makes a man drunk, sinks him into forgetfulness, so also the recollection of God and of his kingdom, when it fills man, makes him forget all sensible things.[1]

Within this climate, the concept of any kind of formal relationship with God is lost. The man who feels the love of God refers his whole existence to him. He lives with God, moves for God, thinks about God. His referral to God constitutes his deepest existential fact, which colors all his particular expressions and activities. Not even this referral is an individual affair, but an event which is completed "in fellowship" within the body of Christ, the Church. Man, as a member of the Church, within the framework of his daily life and relationships with his neighbor and the world, is renewed and transformed. Thus the urging of the Apostle Paul is realized: "Whether you eat, then, or drink of act, do everthing to the glory of God" (1 Cor 10.31).

Man's reference to God has already been realized essentially in Christ. But this same reference is repeated liturgically in the celebration of the Holy Eucharist. The Holy Eucharist is the Liturgy in which the faithful is called to function by referring himself together with the others to God: " . . . let us commit ourselves, one another, and our whole life to Christ our God."[2] Thus the Divine Liturgy is and remains the center and goal of the life of the faithful and of the Church.

All the day and night services by which the Church refers the world and time to God are celebrated with the Divine Liturgy as the center and pinnacle. The Liturgy is a communion of God with the world. It is a participation in the joy of the resurrection which is fulfilled in the Holy Communion. The Christian who participates in the Church's Liturgy and extends it into his life shares in the liturgical reference of himself and the world to God.

The Holy Eucharist is not an unrepeatable sacrament, but a sacrament which is performed continuously "for the life of the world." That is why the faithful are called to approach the Holy Communion regularly. The philosopher and martyr, Justin, informs us that in his time (second century A.D.) Christians communicated every Sunday.[3] We have comparable information from other writers and Fathers of the Church as well. But in addition, as Saint Basil the Great informs us, many Christians were accustomed to communicate even on weekdays.

In particular, Wednesday, Friday and Saturday were dedicated as days for the celebration of the Divine Liturgy in addition to Sunday, as was any other day on which the Church celebrated the memory of some saint. All the Christians who attended communicated at every Liturgy. The Church did not separate attendance at the Divine Liturgy from approaching the Holy Communion. For every faithful who attended the Divine Liturgy, it was self-evident that he would approach the Holy Communion unless he had some canonical impediment which prevented him.

Since Christians communicated so often, the so called Presanctified Liturgies were instituted which are still celebrated today, every Wednesday and Friday of Lent, since it is not permitted to celebrate the Divine Liturgy on the weekdays of Lent, as is well known. Therefore, the Presanctified Liturgies are performed with the consecrated bread and the consercrated wine of the previous Sunday, and it became possible in this way for the faithful to communicate even on these two days.

Of course, in our days, this habit of regular Holy Communion is not so well known to Christians. Today, only the priest who celebrate and a few Christians communicate every Sunday or on other days of the week. But why is this phenomenon observed? Is it because today's Christians are or feel themselves to be unworthy to communicate regularly? Is it because they don't even know that they can? Or finally, is it because they are indifferent and therefore limit themselves to communicating only a few times a year?

If we try to examine the facts closely, we only will see that each of the reasons to which we have referred, or even all of them together sometimes, keep Christians far from the Holy Communion. There is, therefore, a serious need to confront this problem.

To begin, we must note that most Christians today who do not communicate very often say that they are unworthy. But by remaining in this condition and communicating two of three times a year, they do not correct the facts. In the time of Saint John Chrysostom, there were many who communicated one or two times a year, because they considered themselves unworthy, and they thought that in this way they were made right with God. But as Chrysostom observes,

> To approach once a year does not deliver us from our crimes, if we approach unworthily. Indeed, it condemns us more, because we do not even approach clearly when we do approach![4]

Purity of heart in the faithful is a condition for the Holy Communion. If someone has his heart pure, in other words, if he has love for God and his neighbor, if he does not feel malice toward other men but always tries to be reconciled with those who do him wrong, if he confesses and receives absolution from his spiritual father, he can and must communicate regularly. But if he does not have his heart pure, if he preserves malice and hatred for any of his fellow men at all, if he forgets the love which God has shown him and taught him, if he is indifferent to his moral condition and does not think of repentance and confession, then he will not correct affairs by communicating two or three times a year.

But there are enough who could approach the Holy Communion more frequently, but they think it is not right. It happens rather often that even clergy are ignorant of the fact that a true Christian who is concerned for his spiritual life, not only can, but should — always, of course, with the permission of his spiritual father to whom he confesses — communicates regularly. Therefore, we need to understand the importance of frequent Holy Communion, to understand that the Divine Liturgy is for Christians to communicate and not for them not to communicate, so that matters will return to their proper path.

Of course, there is the third reason to which we have referred, that is indifference to the frequent approach to the Holy Communion. The truth is that this reason is also the most frightening. The sinner can repent; he who does not know can be taught; but the one who is indifferent has little hope of being saved. The greatest and most difficult work for us is to confront this indifference — indifference to the frequent approach to the Holy Communion, and more generally, indifference to the Christian life and faith.

Indifference, which in the language of the monks is characterized as spiritual boredom and is considered as a deadly sin, constitutes the principle obstacle to the spirtual life. The one who is indifferent is a Christian who does not know what it means to be a Christian. Still more, he is a sinner who does not feel his sinfulness and so is not led to repentance. He is indifferent to everything and thinks that everything is going well.

But this is the worst state for a Christian. It is the heaviest form of sickness in the area of spiritual life. Unfortunately, this spiritual sickness is seen very widely in our time, almost in the form of an epidemic. The conventionalism of contemporary man's religious faith, the laxity of moral life, the dulling of the spiritual senses is so widespread today that while we are now in an especially critical state, we do not even understand it.

Therefore then, it is necessary to struggle against this indifference, this spiritual boredom, which is killing man spiritually. For this struggle to be effective, it must begin from our own selves. Because we all have fallen, more or less, into this fearful sickness of indifference. If we do not fight this sickness within our own selves, our efforts for others cannot prosper.

But how can this happen? This question takes us back to the point from which we began. For the spirit of indifference, which sometimes more, sometimes less, attacks the faithful, to be defeated, and for the power of faith to be revealed, the benevolence of God must become conscious before us and our gratitude before him must be cultivated. In this way, the conditions are created for rendering true worship to God. So long as worship is the heart of Christian life, the best conditions exist for Christian life to develop.

The liturgical wealth of our Church helps in precisely this effort. The wise arrangement of the feasts and services within ecclesial time, the magnificent hymns and the readings, the brilliant architecture and adornment of our Byzantine churches, the wonderful Byzantine icons, whose value we have at last begun to understand — these are the best aids and guides on the road of true faith and worship of God.

Certainly there are enough difficulties to understand and value, as we should, this great treasure of ours. The rhythm of contemporary life is very different from that of our ancestors. The haste and nervousness of our time come into opposition to the quiet and peaceful spirit of the life and worship of our Church. The language of our time is very different from the languaage in which her texts and hymns are written. The icons which we have used or even still use sometimes today in our houses or in our churches do not have the grace and the holy fitness of the ancient byzantine icons, but derive from a western environment which is foreign to the orthodox tradition. Very many difficulties appear in our attempt to know and live orthodox life and worship better. But transcending all this, there is always the possibility of success, a possibility which can be transformed into reality by our will and love.

The Divine Liturgy of Saint Basil the Great

"Prayer of the Holy Offering,"
also called "The Holy Anaphora" (Extract)

O you who truly exist, Master, Lord, God, Father, Almighty: it is truly fitting and right and worthy at the majesty of your holiness to praise you, to sing to you, to bless you, to worship you, to give thanks to you, to glorify you who alone are truly God; to offer you with a broken heart and in a spirit of humility this our reasonable worship; for it is you who has granted us the knowledge of your truth. Who is able to tell of your might and to make your praises heard, or to describe all your wonderful works in every time? O Master of all, Lord of heaven and earth and of all creation, visible and invisible, you who are enthroned on the throne of glory, who look upon the abyss, Eternal One, invisible, beyond understanding indescribable, unchangeable, the Father of our Lord Jesus Christ the great God and Savior and our hope. For he is the image of your goodness, your identical imprint, revealing you the Father in himself; he is the living Word, the true God, the Wisdom from eternity life, sanctification, power, the true light through whom the Holy Spirit shone forth, the Spirit of truth, the gift of adoption, the pledge of the pledge of the future inheritance, the first-fruits of eternal goods, the life-giving power, the fountain of sanctification. Empowered by him, every reasonable and intelligent creature serves you and sends up eternal glory, for all things are your servants. For angels, archangels, thrones, dominions, princedoms, authorities, powers and the many-eyed cherubim praise you. The Seraphim stand in a circle about you, one with six wings and another with six wings, who cover their faces with two, and their feet with two, and fly with two, crying to one another, with unresting voices and unceasing praise . . .

NOTES

[1] A mind that has found spiritual wisdom is like a man who finds a fully equipped ship at sea, and once he has gone aboard, it brings him from the sea of this world to the isle of the age to come. In like manner, the perception of the future age while in this world is like an islet in the ocean; and he who approaches it toils no longer amind the billows of the appearances of this age." Saint Isaac the Syrian, *Homily* 48, p. 231.

[2] "The Litany of Peace," sung by the deacon.

[3] *Apology* 1.67.3-5.

[4] *Against the Anomoians* 6, PG 48.755.

CHAPTER NINE

The Spiritual Father
and the Brothers in Christ

Christ who reveals God the Father to man at the same time reveals the right relationship of man with God the Father. He reveals this relationship, not only by his teaching, but also by his own presence in the world as Son of God and redeemer of man. As Son of God he is indissolubly united with God the Father: "I and the Father are one" (Jn 10.30). He comes into the world to fulfil the will of the Father (Jn 6.38), and he fulfils the Fathers' will by offering himself "for the life of the world" (Jn 6.51).

Without Christ no one can approach the Father (Jn 14.6), but whoever knows Christ also knows the Father. Whoever sees Christ

80

sees the Father: "If you knew me, you would also know the Father. And from now on you do know him and have seen him . . . whoever has seen me has seen the Father" (Jn 14.7-9). At the same time, however, by revealing the love of God the Father to men and offering his life for their salvation and renewal, Christ is revealed himself as Father of the new life of men.

This paternal property of Christ, which has almost been forgotten in recent theology, is fundamental to a correct consideration of the divine fatherhood. Christ, who is the new Adam and the Father of the new life of men, has no earthly father, but only an earthly mother, the Virgin. This means that in the new creation, which is inaugurated with the coming of Christ into the world, earthly fatherhood is abolished and virginal motherhood is introduced. The fatherhood of the old Adam, which was defeated by death, is replaced by the fatherhood of the new Adam, who conquers death, while the motherhood of Eve, which transmitted death, is replaced by the motherhood of the Most Holy Virgin who bears life.

It is characteristic, however, that Christ reveal the divine fatherhood to men as their brother. He does not impose any external authority; but, as the "first-born of many brothers" (Rom 8.29), he takes his brothers into his own body and presents, them to his heavenly Father. Earthly fatherhood is replaced by heavenly fatherhood and natural motherhood by virginal motherhood, that is, by the birth of man into the body of the Church, which is itself the body of Christ, the body which he assumed at his incarnation by the Virgin Mary. Thus, man is freed from death and becomes a participant in eternal life.

In this new life, the unity of Christ with the Father constitutes the paradigm of the unity of the faithful among themselves. This is, moreover, the petition of the Lord's high priestly prayer: "That all may be one, Father, as you are in me and I in you, that they may be one in us" (Jn 17.21). This unity, which is offered to the faithful as a gift of the Triadic God and makes them brothers, constitutes at the same time the petition which the faithful are called to live in their everyday life. It is what is given by, and at the same time, what is sought from their participation in the body of Christ.

Faith, then, in Christ offers the faithful brotherly relations with all the members of the Church. When the Christian lives this faith of his, he also lives his brotherly relations with the other Christians.

By the power of the divine fatherhood and with the mystery of virginal motherhood, the new race of men is inagurated, the race of the children of God. Men are unified by the fatherhood of the heavenly Father, which sets aside every earthly fatherhood: "Call no one on earth your father, for your Father is one" (Mt 23.9). Any earthly fatherhood whatever is conventional and unimportant before the heavenly fatherhood. That is, the recognition of God the Father, essentially sets aside every earthly fatherhood, not only physical but also spiritual, God is the only Father of men and only to him does the name of Father belong by right.

At the same time, however, God is he "from whom every fatherhood in heaven or on earth is named" (Eph 13.15). This means that even earthly fatherhood can exist. But this finds its meaning and its value, when it is included in the perspective of the heavenly fatherhood, when it helps man to know or to preserve the heavenly fatherhood. Therefore, even spiritual fatherhood, the highest form of earthly fatherhood, is considered by the Church as a symbol of the divine fatherhood. The spiritual father exists in the Church as a type or symbol of God.

The Orthodox tradition especially emphasizes the need for the existence of spiritual fathers to direct the faithful in the spiritual life. For monastics, the spiritual father is another monk, the "elder" (*gerontas*), while for the laity, he is a priest in the world or perhaps again a monastic "elder." The elder is not necessarily advanced in years, but he is experienced in the spiritual life. He is a man who can offer, not so much ethical teaching, as a way of life. In the person of the spiritual father, the faithful see Christ himself, who is also their real Father. His love for Christ is manifest by his love for his spiritual father.

In contemporary society, the concept of the spiritual father has almost been forgotten, while the concept of the father in general has been blackened and falsified. So, this concept has even been connected with oppression and tyranny. Correspondingly, the revolt against the father, whether in the person of our natural parents or in the person of any higher cleric of layman whatever, has reached a peak, This situation assuredly impedes man's reference to God the Father.

In the person of Christ and in his relationship with God the Father, man finds true fatherhood and the true content of the relations of a son with his father. In opposition to every concept of oppression or tyranny with which the concept of the father has been connected, fatherhood appears in the economy in Christ as an unlimited self-offering of the love of the Father to the Son, and sonship as an unlimited self-abandonment of the Son to the will of the Father. God the Father offers everything to the Son (Jn 13.2,16.15). But the Son acts entirely in accord with the will of the Father (Mt 26.30; Jn 5.30; 6.38). Christ as man does not cease to have his human will as well. But this will of his is completely submitted to his divine will, as is his human activity in general to his divine activity.

Christ, who revealed God the Father to the world and was himself revealed as father and brother of man, does not remain outside the life of the faithful, but approaches them in the specific form of the spiritual father and brother. But again, it must not be forgotten that the spiritual father is, at the same time, also a spiritual brother. If Christ, who is the God and creator of man, does not impose his divine fatherhood as an external authority, but reveals it with love as a brother of man, even more the spiritual father, who is a creature and child of God, must not act otherwise. This is how the Fathers of the Church have seen and cultivated spiritual fatherhood.

The spiritual father is a brother in Christ of his spiritual children; he must sacrifice himself for his spiritual children. He even reaches the point of not wanting to be saved without his spiritual children. "I have seen yet another," writes Saint Symeon the New Theologian, having himself in mind,

> who was so zealous and filled with desire for the salvation of his brethren that he often implored God, who loves man, with all his soul and with warm tears that either they might be saved or else that he be condemned with them. His attitude was like that of Moses

and indeed of God himself in that he did not in any way wish to be saved alone. Because he was spiritually bound to them by holy love in the Holy Spirit, he did not want to enter into the kingdom of heaven itself if it meant that he would be separated from them."[1]

Paternal love unites the spiritual father with his spiritual children. And the response of the spiritual child to the love of the spiritual father maintains his unity with him and with his spiritual brothers. The spiritual child offers his will freely to the will of his spiritual father and so finds the freedom and universality of his person in the universality of his free self-offering. As Abba Dorotheos notes,

> He who does not have his own will always does his own will, because whatever might happen satisfies him and he is always found doing his own will. For he does not want things to become as he want· them, but he wants them as they are.[2]

Finally, all alike, spiritual father and spiritual children, are brothers among themselves, because they are children of Christ, who became a brother to mankind and established them as children of God the Father. Thus, spiritual fatherhood serves the brotherhood in Christ and the spiritual brotherhood emerges from the experience of adoption in Christ.

The ideal form of spiritual fatherhood is cultivated in the monastic community. But this does not mean that such relationships cannot be cultivated in the wider ecclesial community as well. Every ecclesial community is formed around the priest, who is also the spiritual father of the faithful. "The Church is a body of which the superior is head.[3] The superior's place is the place of the place of a spiritual father. Obedience to him has the sense of obedience to Christ. And the common obedience to Christ, which is made specific by obedience to the spiritual father, cultivates the brotherhood of the faithful. Finally, this obedience leads the faithful to real freedom, because it sets them free from the despotism of their own selves which provokes the most intense form of slavery for man.

To be sure, the property of the spiritual father is not constituted by any administrative or bureaucratic office; rather, it is spiritual function. This property assumes the communion of the Holy Spirit. Without the communion of the Holy Spirit, there cannot be a spiritual fatherhood, just as there cannot even be a spiritual brotherhood or a spiritual life in general. Objectification of the charismatic life and formalization of the spiritual ralationships of the faithful are alien to the life of the Church and extinguish its grace.Therefore, the presence of true spiritual fathers who cultivate the spiritual life of the faithful and preserve their community alive by the grace of the Holy Spirit has capital importance for the Church. Without these fathers, the life of the faithful is hopelessly impoverished and dies. In the opposite way, it is enriched by their pressence and renewal.

On the other hand, the brotherhood of mankind in Christ is created by their common inclusion in the body of Christ and their adoption in Christ into God the Father. As is well-known, the Christians of the first centuries felt themselves to be and addressed one another as brothers. This brotherhood in Christ was placed more highly natural brotherhood. Certainly with the institutionalization of the Church and the objectification of spiritual relationships in religious life, this concept lost ground. The phrase "brother in Christ," which is preserved in ecclesial language, is usually used in order to indicate more formal relationships among Christians or especially ecclesiastical officers. But it is noteworthy that this phrase usually reappears in charismatic groups and "born-again" religious circles in order to characterize the relationship of the members to one another. More generally, however, wherever true faith in Christ is cultivated, brotherly relations automatically develop among the faithful, or wherever this faith is revealed, the brotherhood in Christ is revealed among the faithful.

But for the Christian, his brothers are not only the brothers in Christ, that is, those who belong to the same Church as him, but all men. Christ, who is the Father and brother of Christians, is simultaneously the Son united indivisibly with the Father, the Lord Almighty: "Because everything is created in him, things in the heavens and things in earth, visible and invisible . . . all things were created through him and for him; and he is before all, and everything is established in him" (Col 1.17). All things, then, belong to Christ, and all men are his creatures. If they do not become or do not remain his children as well, it is something that grieves the Christian but without causing him to lose hope. His love toward them as a manifestation of his love for the common Father and Creator of World, cannot be anything but true and unqualified.

"The person who loves God," says Saint Maximos the Confessor, "cannot help loving every man as himself, even though he is grieved by the passions of those who are not yet purified. But when they amend their lives, his delight is indescribable and knows no bounds.[4]

The love of the true Christian cannot be limited to any framework at all, but overflows without limit in order to embrace the entire world, the entire creation. It is manifested as "the heart's burning for the sake of the entire creation, for men, for birds, for amimals, for demons, and for every created thing."[5]

This brotherly love for other men is not some abstract theological of social concept, but a concrete relationship with concrete human persons in everyday life. The Christian's brother is the particular person with whom he associates, converses and beside whom he works, not an abstract concept of man or humanity. The truth of the Christian brotherhood is a personal truth. Its experience is authentic only in the area of the personal relationship and society. To detach the concept of brotherhood from concrete human persons leads easily, not only to its alienation, but also to its complete falsification.

Abba Dorotheos: Letter 2

"To the superiors and disciples of the monastery,
how the superiors must admonish the brothers and
how the novices must submit to those who teach them."[6]

1. If you are superior of brothers, care for them with strictness of heart and compassionate mercy, teaching them by word and deed what they must do, but more by deed since examples are more effective. Become an example for them, whether you are strong in body or whether you are weak, by the good state of your soul and with

the fruits of the Spirit which are enumerated by the Apostle — love, joy, peace, patience, honesty, kindness, faith, humility and self — restraint from all the passions (v. Gal 5.22-23).

Do not be excessively angry over the slips which happen, but calmly point out the harm which derives from the slip. If it is necessary to reprove someone, do it observing who the person is and when would be an apt occasion. Do not be too exacting about small mistakes as though you were scrupulous yourself, nor be criticizing constantly, for this is burdensome. The habits of the critic lead to insensitivity and contempt. Do not command in a haughty manner, but counsel the brother with humility, for this manner of speech will stimulate him and persuade him more and give comfort to the neighbor.

2. At a time of trouble when a brother resists you, hold tongue lest you say something in anger. Do not let your heart be raised against him, but remember that he is your brother and a member in Christ and an image of God who has been influenced by our common enemy. Have compassion on him lest the devil capture him by the hurt of anger and kill him by resentment and his soul, for which Christ died (1 Cor 8.11) be destroyed by your carelessness. Remember also that you are subject to the same sin of anger, and in your weakness sympathize with your brother and give thanks that you have found ground to forgive him, so that you also may be forgiven more and greater things by God. "Forgive," he says, "and you will be forgiven" (Lk 6.37; Mt 6.14). Do you think that your brother is harmed by your patience? But the Apostle Paul commends us to conquer evil with good, not evil with evil (Rom 12.11) and the Fathers say, "If you are moved to anger when you are reproving another, you have given effect to the same passion."[7] No one is so foolish as to tear down his own house in order to build one for his neighbor!

3. If the trouble persists, constrain your heart, and pray speaking in this way:

O God who loves mankind and who is the lover of our souls, who in your unspeakable goodness brought us into existence from nonexistence (cf. Rom 4.17) in order to share in your goods, and who recalls us through the blood of your only Son our Savior when rebel against your commandments: Now be present in our weakness and reprimand the turmoil in our hearts as once you did the stormy sea (cf. Mt 8.26). Do not be bereft of us both at one time (cf. Gen 27.45) by our being put to death by sin nor say to us, "What benefit is there in my blood, and in my descent into corruption?" (Ps 29.10) and "Amen, I say to you, I do not know you" (Mt 25.12). because our lamps have gone out from a lack of oil (Mt 25.8).

4. After this prayer, when your heart has been soothed, you can then reprove, rebuke, plead and with sympathy heal and correct him with wisdom and humility, as a sick member in accord with the apostolic precept (2 Tim 4.2). For then the brother will receive correction with intelligence and accuse himself for his hardness and through your peace you will pacify his heart. Let nothing, then, separate you from the holy tradition of Christ who says: "Learn of me, for I am lowly and humble in heart" (Mt 11.29). For it is necessary to attend first to a peaceful condition, so that the heart not become confused either by fair suggestions or because of a so-called commandment, persuaded that we fulfil all the commandments because of love and purity of heart. If you govern your brother in this way, you will hear the voice saying, "If you derive something valuable from what is worthless, you will be my mouth" (Jer 15.19).

5. If you are under obedience, never trust your own heart, for it is blind from its old inclinations. Do not follow your own judgment in anything and do not decide anything yourself without asking advice. Do not consider yourself or regard your opinions as more easy or more fair than those of your superior. Do not become an examiner of his works and often a deceived tester, for this is an illusion of the evil one intended to obstruct you from obedience with faith in all things and from the salvation assured by this. Submit with contentment and you will advance in the way of the Fathers without danger and without error. Constrain yourself in all things and cut off your will, and by the grace of Christ you will become habituated to cutting it off through practice and in future you will do it without effort of pain, as it will always happen to be your own will. "For you do not want things to be as you wish, but you want them as they are," and thus you are at peace with everything[8] — everything indeed, which does not transgress a commandment of God or the Fathers.

Struggle to find in everything a ground to reproach yourself and maintain disinterestedness in your awareness. Believe that what relates to us in the smallest detail is by the providence of God, and you will bear whatever comes to you undisturbed. Believe that disgrace and insults are medicines for the pride in your soul pray for those who abuse you as true doctors, persuaded that he who hates disgrace hates humility and that he who flees those who provoke him flees lowliness.

Do not desire to know your neighbor's fault nor accept suspicions about him; and if suspicions spread because of our wickedness, take care to change them into a good understanding. Give thanks in everything and you will acquire goodness and holy love.

6. Above all, let us all guard our conscience in all things directed both to God and, in material concerns, to our neighbor. Before we say or do something, let us examine it to see if it is according to the will of God, and praying in this way, let us speak of act. Let us cast our weakness before God, and his goodness will accompany us in all things.

NOTES

[1] *The Discourses* 8,56-64, tr. C. J. deCatanzaro (New York, 1980), p. 144-5. See also Abp. Basil Krivochcheine, *In the Light of Christ*, tr. Anthony Gythiel (Crestwood, 1981), p. 94.

[2] "Various Brief Sayings," PG 88.1810BC. *Essays and Letters*, ed. Aikaterina Goltsou (Thessalonike, 1986), in the series *Philokalia of the Watchful and Ascetical Fathers* 12. p. 646.

[3] Saint Symeon the New Theologian, *Discourses* 18.345-6, tr. C.J. deCatanzaro, (New York, 1980), pp. 144-45.

[4] *Texts on Love* 1.13, *Philokalia* 2, 54.

[5] Saint Isaac the Syrian, *Homily* 71, p. 344.

[6] Tr. from Abba Dorotheos, *Essays and Letters*, ed. Aikaterina Goltsou (Thessalonike, 1986), in the series *Philokalia of the Watchful and Ascetical Fathers* 12, p. 646.

[7] *Apophthegmata*, Makarios 17, PG 65.269B.

[8] Epiktetos, *Manual* 9.

CHAPTER TEN

The Commemoration
of the Saints

Saints are those grace-filled men and women who emptied themselves by their humility and love for Christ in order to find it again in the person of Christ and their neighbor. They are those who conquered their self-love and let the grace of God be revealed in their existence. They are the members of the body of Christ who reveal the presence of Christ himself in the world. The Church honors the saints and proposes their lives for the spiritual guidance and edification of the faithful.

The *Lives* of the saints constitute the *Synaxaria*,[1] so called because they are read at the religious gatherings (Gk: *synaxis*) of the faithful. These texts with their narratives of a style of life, in which human self-love has been conquered and the grace of God revealed, have always had a special place in the Orthodox Church. The faithful are nurtured daily by them in their spiritual life. Especially during the period of Turkish rule, the *Synaxaria* were the favorite reading of the oppressed Orthodox race. Therefore, it is somewhat disturbing that these texts are being put aside in modern times. Certainly, it is true that contemporary man with his individualistic and rationalistic spirit finds it difficult to accept these texts. In fact, the *Synaxaria* contain amazing and surprising material which often provokes a reaction from the rationalist or individualist of our time. But at the same time, they provide the means for a substantive and general reflection on life, something which is especially needed by contemporary man.

Life, as Saint Athanasios observes, is connected with motion. "We say that the body is alive when it moves and that its death occurs when it ceases to move."[2] The science of government today combines life with information. "I live" means "I receive information." An enormous wave of information, the greatest amount of which has its beginning in our own body, unceasingly reaches our brain in order to stimulate appropriate responses by it. Most of this information is unconscious and does not detain us. Conversely, the information which our senses transfer from the external world, especially sight and hearing, occupies our attention more.

But outside of the information which we gather by ourselves, there are the so-called communication media which supply us with assembled information. Such media are the newspapers, radio, television. We all read newspapers, listen to the radio or watch television. Indeed, most are accustomed to follow these media at regular times of the day. If, then, we were to ask someone what he finds of interst, he would usually answer, "Well, nothing in particular." But yet every information bulletin or page of the newspaper reports so many important events about the people and things around us which disturb our fellows — wars, massacres, deaths, suicides, tortures, crimes, accidents, etc. — that if someone wished to live or even to feel these events personally, he would be in danger of going mad. He slips over them or is temporarily moved but later forgets them. He separates himself from the misery which, he has been told, exists around him and entrenches himself behind a dullnes and indifference to the world's misfortune. But the last taste which remains from all this is a taste of emptiness. The newspaper, the most representative means of presenting the events of the day with the great pain and agony which they can conceal, is a purely ephemeral text. The next day we are usually in a hurry to throw it out or get rid of it. It no longer has anything in particular to say to us.

The *Synaxarion* is a kind of newspaper. It is the "newspaper" of our Church. A few contemporary Christians speak with some reserve about this book, as they do about the faithful who read it. Others limit themselves to stressing the value of the Holy Scriptures and consider involvement with texts such as those of the *Synaxarion* to be superfluous. Naturally, no one can disregard the value of the Holy Scriptures. But within the Church, they are approached with the aid of the saints. Just as no one can approach Christ without the saints who are members of his body, so no one can approach even the word of Christ, the Gospel, without the aid which the saints offer. The lives of the saints are living commentaries on the Gospel in the history of the Church.

The *Synaxarion* is not a newspaper to be thrown away or set aside. It is the journal which is continually valid and returns to us again. Starting from the momentary and transient, it moves to the eternal and indestructible. It does this by ceaselessly presenting us with the eternal and indestructible body of Christ, which is the saints. We see this body in the *Synaxarion* every day in a particular form. As an example, we cite the text for April 15:[3]

On the fifteenth [of April], the commemoration of the holy martyr Crescens:

> It was astonishing to see Crescens in the midst of the fire, considering the flame as a pleasant meadow. In the fierce fire, Crescens died on the fifteenth.

He was from Myra in Lycia from a brilliant and famous family, old and advanced in age. He saw that impiety had reached a peak, that the religion of idols stood proud, and that there were many enslaved to error and offering sacrifices to the lifeless wooden statues. Moved by zeal, this blessed man went into the midst of the idolaters and admonished them to depart from this deceit, to turn to God, in whom Christians believe and who is the creator of every spirit and giver of all life.

Then the governor called the saint wretched and unfortunate, because he wished to undergo torture willingly; therefore, the saint replied to him, that for someone to suffer for Christ is a cause of happiness and bliss. The governor asked him what his name was and his native land, but the saint gave only one answer to all the questions, that is, that he was a Christian. Thus, he disdained to appear to offer reverence to idols even in the smallest detail, as the governor was advising him, but he confessed God who is over everything before them all. He also said that the body could not do anything else than what the soul wished, since it is moved and governed by the soul. Then, because of what he said, first the saint was first hung and torn, then a great fire was lit and he was thrown into it; but the fire did not even harm a hair of his head. Wherefore giving thanks, he commited his soul into the hands of God, from whom he received the crown for his feat.

On the same day, the commemoration of the holy martyrs, the women Anastasia and Vasilissa:

> They slew two lambs of the lamb of God, Anastasia and Vasilissa together.

These saints were noble and rich and bore the honor of being students of the Holy Apostles Peter and Paul who were executed by Nero. After their death, they took their honorable and apostolic relics at night and buried them. In the year 56, during the reign of Nero, they were brought down from the great city of Rome. Since they had become known to the impious Nero, they were before him. First they were thrown in prison; then, when they had been asked if they would deny the faith of Christ and they had anwered that they persist in it, they were hung. Then their breasts, hands, feet and tongues out off, and finally their heads. Thus, the blessed women went up to heaven wearing their crowns [of martyrdom].

The holy martyr Leonidas, bishop of Athens, was brought to his end in peace:

> Sudden darkness oppressed Athens, when her sun, Leonidas, set on her.

The holy martyrs Theodore, the priest, and Pausolypios were put to death by the sword:

> For Pausolypios and Theodore, the sacrificer's sword was truly a gift, ending their pain.[4]

Through the intercessions of your saints, Christ our God, have mercy on us.

In this text are commemorated six saints: four men and two women. All are martyrs. Among them are a bishop and a priest. In the readings for the following day are commemorated sixteen saints; the day after, six by name and 1150 anonymous saints. More generally, in the *Synaxarion*, reference in made to saints known by name or anonymous, monastics, martyrs, apologists, confessors, etc. This variety in the members of the body of Christ outlines the special shape and the special character of each day of the ecclesiastical year. The variety of afflictions, tortures, martyrdoms, struggles, spiritual discipline conceals — and often more than conceals — the pain which we live, which we see, which we know, which we feel. A pain gathered, but also conquered in the name of Christ, within his own body, the Christ.

The first saint of the day in the text which we have cited is Saint Crescens. He comes from Myra in Lycia, where impiety and idolatry had reached a peak.

On the sixth of December, we have the commemoration of a great bishop of the same city, Saint Nickolas. During the period of his priesthood (episcopate) — at the beginning of the fourth century and obviously later than the time of Crescens — a great number of Christians were in the city. Many of them were arrested with Saint Nickolas, tortured and thrown into prison, to be freed by the Edict of Milan proclaiming religious toleration (313 A.D.)

Crescens is characterized by the governor of the place with two words: "wretched" and "unfortunate." He is described this way, "because he wished to undergo torture willingly."

To this characterization, which expresses the world's understanding and evaluation of the facts, we have the saint's response which expresses the Christian or theological view: For someone to suffer for Christ is a cause of happiness and bliss."

One of the beatitudes of the Lord says: "Blessed are you when they revile you and persecute you and speak every kind of slander against you, lying because of me. Rejoice and be glad, for your reward is great in heaven" (Mt 5.11-12). The attitude of the saint's words here provides an empirical proof of this blessing of Christ.

A usual feature in the *Lives* of the saints is the miracles. Reading them, one sees many and varied miracles. The most general, however, and greatest miracle which the saints present is the willing acceptance of pain an death. They endure the tortures and perform miracles for others.

Here, the saint comes willingly to be tortured. Since he suffers in seeing the height of idolatry, he presents himself to the idolaters and urges them to believe in God. From the history of the Church, we also have other cases for a more direct examination of martyrdom. There is the well-known phenomenon of rushing in that, is, the willing approach to martyrdom, which was finally prohibited by the Church.

This attitude comes into opposition with human habit. Man flees pain and pursues pleasure. Here, the facts are reversed. We have an acceptance of pain and its transformation into spiritual pleasure. The saint is free from natural, wordly, or social bonds. His existence is not identified with his body, and so his acts are not chosen or determined by the criterion of the pleasure or pain which can be produced in him. The saint's existence is in the body of Christ, where every real Christian's existence belongs. That is the meaning of Baptism and participation in the Holy Eucharist.

Thus we understand the purpose for which the *Lives* of the saints, the *Synaxaria*, were written. Their purpose is to present the individual events in the lives of the saints. These are incidents which come and pass away. It is these which can be written in the newspapers to in-form and satisfy human curiosity. Their purpose is to reveal man's existence in Christ. Therefore, the *Synaxarion* is not concerned especially with the historical accuracy of the particular events. It does not have the spirit of Thucydides at all, which investigates the truth of the individual conscience, but it is concerned to present the unity of the fragmented elements within the dimensions of the ecclesial body. The Byzantine chronicles share the same spirit.

What meaning can the objects and events have independent of man? All possess a sense and existence in relation to man, or rather, in relation to the sense which man finds in them. Here, the saints constitute pointers for the life of the faithful within the world. For our time, this is especially so of the new martyrs and contemporary saints.

The saints reveal the meaning which communion with Christ has for the life of man. They reveal the truth of the christification of man. This is shown here in the simple and unaffected behavior of Saint Crescens. When asked by the governor to tell his name and his homeland, he monotonously gave him the same answer, that he is a Christian. The same thing exists in the patristic tradition and as a theological teaching.

Saint Gregory of Nyssa presents the meaning of the name "Christian" for the faithful analytically in his essay, *On Perfection*[5] The writer notes especially the following:

> Our good Master has granted us fellowship in the greatest, most divine and first of all names, so that those who have become worthy of bearing the name of Christ are called Christians. It would seem necessary, then that all the terms that describe such a name be perceived in us as well, so that what we are called should not be falsely attributed to us, but rather have its evidence in our life. For *to be* something does not come about from being called that; but the underlying nature of something, whatever it happens to be, is known through the meaning of the name which fits the nature.[6]

One is a true Christian (and not falsely called a Christian) when this name, given by Christ's grace, epitomizes one's life and existence. Saint Crescens forgets himself, his name, his homeland, and lives

Christ. Christ is his self, his name, his country, his life. He cannot remain closed in his ego and be called Christian. In order to be called Christian, he must resemble Christ. And to resemble Christ, he must not belong to himself but to him who offered himself to man out of love: "For only when we do not belong to ourselves do we become like him who through love has reconciled us to himself."[7]

Man is a creature "in the image and likeness" of God. In order, then, to be authentically human, he must preserve the marks of the image of God, the marks of Christ. The saint who forgets himself for Christ and lives Christ is the authentic human being. It is he who abandons alienation and finds his true existence. He is the creature "in the image and likeness" of God, who has been restored to his rightful place and perspective.

By their self-denial, the saints create a tremendous area of freedom where the world and the things of the world, even in their tragic form, can become playthings and means of recreation. This is expressed wonderfully in the iambic distichs[8] of Christophoros of Mytilene (eleventh century) which are prefixed to the lives of the saints. For Saint Crescens who was tortured and thrown into the fire where he suffered nothing, is notes that he considered the flames as a pleasant meadow. The two women martyrs, Anastasia and Vasilissa, are slaughtered as lambs of the Lamb of God. The death of Saint Leonidas, Bishop of Athens, does not harm him, just as the setting of the sun does not destroy the sun; nevertheless, it sinks Athens immediately into darkness. The name of Pausolypios and the quality of Theodore, who as a priest offered sacrifices to God, give the pretext for a beautiful pun. Such puns are quite frequent in the *Lives* of the saints.

The reading from the *Synaxarion* for the day concludes, as always, with the invocation of the mercy of God: "Through the intercession of your saints, Christ our God, have mercy of us." Some people say: There is but one mediator between God and man, Christ. Why do we seek the intercession of the saints? Even the Holy Scriptures confirm, "For there is one God, and mediator between God and man, the man Christ Jesus, who gave himself as a ransom for all" (1 Tim 2.5-6). But Christ did not come into the world as an angel, but as the Son of the Virgin. The Blessed Virgin, who was made worthy to become the mother of Christ, also made passible his dwelling in every man. We receive Christ because of the Blessed Virgin who was made worthy to give birth to him as man. Again, there remains one God and mediator between God and man, Christ. But this mediation became possible through the Blessed Virgin. Christ saves us as the Son of the Virgin. This leads us to live our salvation by Christ "through the intercessions of the Mother of God."[9] The Mother of God does not redeem us; the Mother of God is not God. But we cannot be redeemed without her; we do not become "participants in the divine nature" (2 Pt 1.4) without the Blessed Virgin.

After the Blessed Virgin come to the saints, those who made themselves a dwelling place for God. When we invoke the saints, we do not invoke new saviors. Seeking their intercessions, we do not seek new mediators. There is one God and mediator, Christ. But when we seek the intercession of the saints, we show our humility and unworthiness, and we beseech God to give us his mercy, not because we are worthy of it, but for the sake of the saints who belong to the body of Christ, in which we also have been included and where we wish to remain in order to be saved.

St. Nikodemos of the Holy Mountain: The New Martyrology[10]

Now, Christians of the present time hear of the martyrdoms and tortures from Church history which the Demitrioses, Georges, Theodores, Jameses and, simply, all the courageous ancient martyrs who were raised up by Christ suffered for his name up until the time of Constantine the Great. They are obliged to believe these things as true, in accord with their duty of simple faith. According to Paul, this faith "is the certainty of things which are not seen" (Heb 11.1). But the antiquity and the great lapse of time which has intervened from then 'til now, can perhaps produce in some, not disbelief, but at least doubt and hesitation. That is, how did they who were men, by nature weak and faint-hearted, endure so much, such appalling and frightful means of punishment? But these new martyrs of Christ, speaking confidently in the theatre of the world, root up all such doubts and hesitations from the hearts of Christians and plant or renew in them unhesitating faith in these martyrs. Just as new food invigorates all those bodies which have been weakened by a previous hunger, just as the early rain revives those trees which were withered from thirst, just as the second growth of feathers renews the aging eagle — "your youth shall be renewed as an eagle" (Ps 102.5) — so also these recently appearing martyrs invigorate, revive, and renew the weakened, withered, and aged faith of present Christians.

Therefore, today's Christians can no longer doubt them. Only with their ears had they heard about those martyrdoms which the ancient martyrs endured. They now see these same things with their eyes, because these new martyrs of Christ endure them. As the common proverb says, the eyes are more trustworthy than the ears. What am I saying, that they only see? Many of today's Christians who are still living have many friends among these newly appearing martyrs. They often ate and drank with them. They were present at their martyrdoms. Their holy blood and clothes were distributed for their blessing, and until now they carry them as talismans, and with their own hands they buried their honorable remains. Thus, they have received precise information about these new martyrs and about the ancient martyrs; or better, they have seen those ancient martyrs in them, because they bear witness even now beneath the face of these new martyrs, and because they appear again in the world as second Georges, second Demitrioses, second Theodores, not just because they have the same names, but rather because their martyrdoms are alike.

But they do not go only this far, but the new martyrs renew the preaching of the holy apostles in the hearts of today's Christians as well; they make the holy Gospel credible and confirm the divinity of Jesus Christ, that he is the true Son of God, consubstantial with the Father who is without beginning, and with his life-giving Spirit, and they preach the great mystery of the Holy Trinity. To put it simply, they set their seal to the whole orthodox faith of Christians, not only with words, but even more with the most terrible forms of punishment which they revived, with their very blood and with their martyrs deaths. Just as Moses' staff of old was first of all a staff, and afterward became a serpent — "and he threw it on the ground, and it became a serpent" (Ex 4.3) — in such a way the faith of Christ, being at first very hot in the time of the apostles and martyrs because of its youth, was changed afterwards into a lukewarm and small faith through age. But just as Moses took the serpent by its last part, or by the tail, and the serpent became a staff — "he extended his hand and took it up by the tail, and it became a staff in his hand" (Ex 4.4) — even so God has set some apart in these last times to become new martyrs, through whom he has again demonstrated the faith, which has risen up for almost two thousand years from us below to Christ himself, years to be warm and youthful, and in this way he has proved them to be a renewal of all the orthodox faith.

NOTES

[1] Books of the lives of saints read daily at Orthros (Matins). — tr.

[2] *Contra Gentes* 33, tr. Robert W. Thomson (Oxford, 1971), p. 91.

[3] Saint Nikodemos of the Holy Mountain, *Synaxarion*, vol. 2, p. 89.

[4] In Greek, this couplet contains a pun on the name Pausolypios and the word *pausilypos* — "ending pain or grief." See also the author's comments below. — tr.

[5] PG 46.251-86 and W. Jaeger (ed.), Gregorii Nysseni, *Opera*, vol. 8.1, pp. 173-214.

[6] PG 46.253D-56A. Jaeger (ed.), p. 177.

[7] Saint Diadochos of Photike, *On Spiritual Knowledge and Discrimination* 4, *Philokalia* 1, 253.

[8] No attempt has been made to reproduce the poetic form of these short verses. — tr.

[9] "Savior, through the intercessions of the Mother of God (Theotokos), save us." 1st Antiphon of the *Divine Liturgy*.

[10] Tr. from the Preface to the 3rd ed. (Athens, 1961), pp. 10-11.

CHAPTER ELEVEN

Faith and Works

Faith constitutes the characteristic mark of the true Christian. Christians are those "who believe" (2 Th 1.10). Christianity is principally "faith" (1 Tim 4.1,6). By faith, the Christian entrusts himself to God, receives the grace of God, and gives his existence worth.

God offers his grace to man initially in Baptism. The grace of Baptism is not offered magically, but sacramentally. No compulsion is exerted on man by this grace, but the possibility of a new life is granted. This life, which was revealed in Christ, becomes accessible to man within the Church. Living as members of the Church, the faithful share in the life of Christ.

The Apostle Paul writes in his Letter to the Thessalonians, "Do not extinguish the Spirit" (1 Th 5.19). This urging has a capital im-

portance for the spiritual life of the faithful. The grace of the Holy
Spirit operates with human consent and cooperation. For grace to
bear fruit, the positive response of man is demanded. His indifference
voids the gift of grace. But whatever positive interest man may have
is vain and fruitless without the grace of God. Therefore, all virtues
and works are characterized by the Apostle Paul as fruit of the Holy
Spirit: "The fruit of the Spirit is love, joy, peace, patience, kindness,
goodness, faithfulness, gentleness, self-control" (Gal 5.22-23). Saint
John Chrysostom interprets this passage of the Apostle Paul writing:

> Why does he call it fruit of the Spirit? Because evil works come from
> us alone, and he therefore calls them works; but the good
> are not due to our diligence only, but also to God's love for man-
> kind.[1]

Man's works acquire sense with faith, but faith is completed by
works. A dichotomy between faith and works is theologically unacceptable. Neither faith without works, nor works without faith give
man worth?[2] The Apostle Paul makes mention of a "work of faith"
(1 Thes 1.3; 2 Thes 1.11) Saint John Chrysostom interprets this phrase
of the Apostle noting that "faith is shown through works."[3] And
Saint Mark the Ascetic in his text, *On Those Who Think That They
Are Made Righteous by Works*, which, with the text of Saint Nickolas
Kabasilas, *The Life in Christ*, gives the most beautiful presentation
of the orthodox teaching about faith and works, writes:

> Some without fulfilling the commandments think that they possess
> true faith. Others fulfil the commandments and then expect the
> kingdom as a reward due to them. Both are mistaken.[4]

When Scripture says "He will reward every man according to his
works" (Mt 16.27), do not imagine that works in themselves merit
either hell or the kingdom. On the contrary, Christ rewards each man
according to whether

> his works are done with faith or without faith in himself; and he
> is not a dealer bound by contract, but God our Creator and
> Redeemer.[5]

There are no works which can make man worthy of the kingdom of God, nor are there works which can make him worthy of Gehenna. What leads man to paradise or to hell are the works of his faith or of his unfaithfulness.

With the works of faith, which comprise words, actions, thoughts, desires, and in general all human dispositions and activities, man becomes a co-worker of God. No human disposition or action whatever has in itself any essential value. Its worthiness or unworthiness depends on its relationship with or its opposition to the grace of God,[6] that is, on whether it expresses faith or faithlessness.

Man is mutable and mortal. Mutability, which is combined with temporality and leads to death, falsifies man and everything human. Here is found the basis for his alienation from the world, from himself, from his works. And so, even the works which could be characterized in themselves as good lose their sense. Still more, these works, when they are realized as works of self-justification, are proved to be detrimental. Luther indicated this truth especially and condemned works which cultivated hypocrisy and boasting.[7] Within the fever of his polemic, however, he went so far as to reject all human cooperation.

Man is called to wrestle with the mutability of his nature, certainly not in order to abolish it, but to place it at the service of the goal of his life. Moreover, mutability itself constitutes the condition for his perfection in goodness.[8] But such and evaluation of mutability is possible only within a body free from decay and death. And this body is the body of Christ, the Church. Any human manifestation or activity which is not clothed in the body of Christ is rendered null. Thus, we are able to understand the word of Christ: "Without me, you can do nothing" (Jn 15.5).

But man cannot remain a non-participant in the work of God for his salvation and renewal. Or, more precisely, this does not bear fruit without his active consent. Saint Nicholas Kabasilas describes the faithful's life in Christ and defines the meaning of his cooperation when he writes:

> There is an element which derives from God, and another which derives from our own zeal. The one is entirely his work, the other

involves striving on our part. However, the latter is our contribution only to the extent that we submit to his grace and do not sur-
render the treasure nor extinguish the torch when it has been
lighted.[9]

What man is called to do is to aspire to remain in the love of
Christ. This is realized by keeping his commandments: "If you keep
my commandments, you remain in my love, as I have kept my Father's
commandments and I remain in his love" (Jn 15. 10). By keeping
the divine commandments, the preservation of the faithful in the love
of God and the increase of the gift of the Holy Spirit in his existence
are also realized. "For it is not enough to love and experience its
passion, but it is necessary as well to persevere in it and to add fuel
to the fire so that it may persist."[10]

Man, then, is not saved by his works, but the grace of God. Much
more, man is not in a position to save others with his own meritorious
works. But on the other hand, man is not saved without his co-
operation in the work of his salvation and renewal, which is evidenced
by keeping the commandments of God. In this case, however, man's
works are nothing else than the self-evident fruit of his faith. Even
Luther accepts good works with this sense. Further, he supports this
position in a homily of his specifically on good works.[11] However,
deriving every good work directly from God and excluding from them
any human cooperation, he is led to the opposite extreme to Roman
Catholicism.

As in many other cases, so here, the Orthodox position on the
relationship of faith to works offers a synthetic transcendence of the
two opposing positions of Protestant and Roman Catholic teaching.
Orthodoxy emphasizes the importance of good works, but without
accepting that these save man or that they increase the grace of God,
as the Roman Catholic Church maintains.[12] But on the other hand,
Orthodoxy considers as good works only the works of faith, again
without ignoring the decided importance of human co-operation. As
Saint Gregory Palamas observes, "For every kind of virtue comes
to us if God is active in us; but, if God is not active in us, everything
that is done by us is sin."[13] Man is not in a position to present good

works without the grace and help of God. But the grace of God cannot bear fruit without the consent and the co-operation of man.

Thus, Orthodox teaching about faith and works can be considered as the mean between the unbridgeable extremes fixed by Protestant and Roman Catholic teaching or as their reconciliation, realized though, on another plane. This other plane shows the most important difference that exists between Orthodox teaching on the one hand and the teaching of the two great branches of the Christian world in the West on the other. Therefore, as is generally the case, it is not difficult to determine that the most important difference within the Christian world is found between the East and West and not between Roman Catholicism and Protestantism. Furthermore, historically, the schism of East asnd West is much more ancient than the schism which was provoked by the reformation.

Roman Catholicism shows a great confidence in phenomena. Nature, man, society, social bonds and, in general, all the data of immediacy are seen as good in themselves. Thus, the whole created world is made autonomous and the kingdom of God is compressed into the framework of the visible Church. On the other hand, Protestantism appears pessimistic in face of the world and of anything wordly. Its teaching, especially about the corruption of human nature (*corruptio naturae*) and the destruction of all kinship with God after the fall excludes the posibility of human co-operation in the work of salvation and renewal. Ultimately, the kingdom of God is projected into a spiritual realm or pushed into an indeterminate future, where only the lordship of God in the world is recognized.

But God is the Lord not only of the future, but also of the present and the past; he is the one "who is and who was and who is to come, the Almighty" (Rev 1.8). The kingdom of God is not located either in phenomena or in what is konwn only by the intellect; he is not defined either in the future or in the present. The kingdom of God, which is "the inheritance of those who are saved," exists after the crucifixion of the senses and the burial of the intellect. It transcends space and is beyond any temporal definition whatsoever: "For it is not right to say that the kingdom of God had a beginning or that it was preceded by ages or by time."[14]

Man's salvation and renewal is not a work of nature, but of grace; it is a fruit of his participation in the uncreated grace of God, that is, in his kingdom, which appeared in Christ and is offered as a gift of the Holy Spirit. Thus, man who is unable to present works worthy of the kingdom of God is granted by God himself to become a participant in his kingdom. The kingdom itself is offered to man in Christ and as a way to the kingdom. The man who receives Christ becomes by the grace of the Holy Spirit a participant in the kingdom of God, while at the same time he walks toward the kingdom. By the light of God he sees the light of God: "In your light, we shall see light" (Ps 35.10).

Man's participation in the kingdom of God is supernatural, because the grace or the kingdom of God, in which man, participates, transcends human nature, "since it does not have that kind of potential in its nature."[15] The basic difference between created and uncreated, between man and God, and created man's natural inability to proceed to the region of the uncreated grace of God, reveal chiefly that man is saved and renewed "freely by his grace" (Rom 3.24).

From this vantage point, Protestantism which stresses that the salvation of man constitutes a gift of God's grace is absolutely correct. Conversely, Roman Catholicism which recognizes a saving value in the works of man diminishes the work of God's grace and maintains clearly Pelagian dispositions which have found their most recent expression in the teaching of Teilhard de Chardin. But on the other hand, Protestantism, by excluding any participation whatever of man in the work of his salvation, excludes as well the communion of man with God and with his saving and renewing grace. Thus, while correctly attributing everything to the grace of God, it maintains a Nestorian separation between it (grace) and man, which has found its extreme expression in contemporary secularization.

Faced with the positions of these two great Christian confessions of the West, Orthodoxy presents its teaching about faith and works as a synthetic transcendence of them, realized, as we have said, on another level. Orthodoxy begins from the basic distinction between created and uncreated, and from their unconfused union in the person of Christ. This union is extended by the grace of the Holy Spirit who assumes and transforms the whole world within the communion of deification, the Church. Thus, Orthodoxy sees man's salvation and renewal as a gift of divine grace, which makes human nature worthy, human nature created "in the image and likeness" of God. Man participates in making his nature worthy by his own consent and by removing the obstacles which oppose the work of divine grace.

Man's contribution, then, to the work of his salvation is limited essentially to the work of receiving and preserving the gift of God: "This alone we contribute to this life — that we submit to his gifts, retain his graces, and do not reject the crown which God by many toils and labors has prepared for us."[16] Man's virtues are cultivated by his participation in the virtue of God. But participation in the virtue of God assumes the denial of the obstacles which man projects to renewal in Christ and which spring from self-love. Freeing himself from self-love, man becomes an acceptable vessel of the grace God and can maintain Christ "living and working" within him. And so, his good works are in reality works of the grace of God. Progress in these works is essentially progress in participation in the grace of God, and progress in participation in the grace of God keeps pace with progress in humility and overcoming self-love.

This position becomes more apparent in Orthodox monasticism, which has as its aim to maximize human co-operation in the work of salvation and renewal.

Monasticism in the West has been closely combined with social activity and service. Throughout the course of its historical development in Roman Catholicism, monastic orders have been formed usually with some specialized activity and mission, while the eremitic life has been put aside and essentially disappeared. Protestantism, from the years of Luther with the publication of his work *De votis monastics,* had already essentially abolished monasticism. This abolition is directly connected with the understanding of Luther, and of the whole protestant world in general, concerning the justification of man. Thus, monasticism which was abolished as an institution was transformed into a generalized form of discipline within the world. But good works, which were rejected as means of buying salvation, were changed into means of its confirmation (*certitudo salutis*).[17]

Conversely, Orthodox monasticism is basically expressive and is not oriented to productive works, but to works of self-emptying. Its chief aim is to combat self-love, which is characterized as the "mother of the passions."[18] Good works are not pursued in themselves, but are combined organically with the struggle against self-love. At the base of every good work and every virtue is located the combat against self-love, or the cultivation of humility, which is characterized as "the beginning and end of virtue" or as "the mother of good deeds."[19]

The discipline which the Christian is called to put into practice in his life and which is institutionalized and intensified particularly in monasticism, has as its aim the struggle against self-love. Self-love, which is defined by Saint Maximos Confessor as the "impassioned, mindless love for one's body,"[20] engages man in the satisfaction of his senses, which lead him from the use of the world to abuse and passion. The Christian, as a member of the body of Christ, does not aim only to return from abuse to use, but extends himself to the development of the divine passion. The intense longing (eros) for sin is changed into an intense longing for God.

This whole course of man's life is simultaneously the expression of his cooperation in the work of his salvation and renewal. In this whole course, mutability appears in man as an invitation of God but at the same time also as an incitement to evil. When mutability is combined with self-love, it leads man to alienation and denial. When, though, it is joined with the grace of God, then it leads to the alteration in accordance with God and perfection:

> Now, the best result of a change is an increase in good things, given always that the change for the better is a change in the one being changed to what is more divine. I say that it is our nature to be mutable — and what I am saying suggests, then, that it is to our detriment that we are not able to accept change for the better, just as it is for a bird which seems afraid to fly to better things.[21]

Mutability, then, within the perspective of the Christian life constitutes a real blessing for man. The span of a human life is not a pointless interval or flow, but a "fit time" or opportunity to value the gifts of God. The destruction of time is the destruction of the "fit time" or opportunity, which is offered by God for salvation and renewal. By his enrolment in the body of Christ, man is called to dedicate himself and his life time to Christ. In this way, he changes his perspective on his mutable nature from one of dissolution and disappearance into one of transfiguration and renewal. The whole course of his life appears as a journey of fulfilment in Christ, which is simultaneously a journey of fulfilment in true freedom. Depending on how immature he is, the faithful will not live in the spirit of freedom in Christ, but will be conformed like a slave to the demands of his faith, and will aim at selfish goals. He does what is good in order to avoid future punishment or to receive a reward. As he proceeds further in his spiritual life, he throws off the spirit of slavery and selfishness. He lives the content of his faith with a spirit of freedom and unselfishness. He understands that God has offered him everything freely from the beginning and that his own co-operation can do nothing more than remove, so far as is possible, what obstructs him in giving effect to and revealing divine grace. God himself acts and is revealed in his existence.

The theme, then, of cooperation must not be considered only in itself, but also in relation to the spiritual condition of the faithful. The man who has some sentiment of the greatness of God's gift knows that even if he offers his whole self, he offers nothing, but simply allows the grace of God to be revealed. His works are not means of negotiation, but of expression. Conversely, whoever is satisfied with his works or supports his hopes on them, does not perceive that God offers him his salvation and renewal freely. Finally, whoever has no care for good works, nor believes that God saves and renews man freely by his grace, cannot be in the communion of the faithful.

Saint Mark the Ascetic
"On Those Who Think That They
Are Made Righteous by Works."[22]

10. Some people when praised for their virtue are delighted, and

attribute this pleasurable feeling of self-esteem to grace. Others when reproved for their sins are pained, and they mistake this beneficial pain for the action of sin.

11. Those who, because of the rigour of their own ascetic practice, despise the less zealous, think that they are made righteous by physical works. But we are even more foolish if we rely on theoretical knowledge and disparage the ignorant.

12. Even though knowledge is true, it is still not firmly established if unaccompanied by works. For everything is established by being put into practice.

13. Often our knowledge becomes darkened because we fail to put things into practice. For when we have totally neglected to practice something, our memory of it will gradually disappear.

14. For this reason Scripture urges us to acquire the knowledge of God, so that through our works we may serve him rightly.

15. When we fulfil the commandments in our outward actions, we receive from the Lord what is appropriate; but any real benefit we gain depends on our inward intention.

16. If we want to do something but cannot, then before God, who knows our hearts, it is as if we have done it. This is true whether the intended action is good or bad.

17. The intellect does many good and bad things without the body, whereas the body can do neither good nor evil without the intellect. This is because the law of freedom applies to what happens before we act.

18. Some without fulfilling the commandments think that they possess true faith. Others fulfill the commandments and then expect the kingdom as a reward due to them. Both are mistaken.

19. A master is under no obligation to reward his slaves; on the other hand, those who serve him well are not given their freedom.

20. If "Christ died on our account in accordance with the Scriptures" (Rom 5.8; 1 Cor 15.3), and we do not "live for ourselves," but "for him who died and rose" on our account (2 Cor 5.15), it is clear that we are debtors to Christ to serve him till our death. How then can we regard sonship as something which is our due?

21. Christ is our Master by virtue of his own essence and Master

by virtue of his incarnate life. For he creates man from nothing, and through His own Blood redeems him when dead in sin; and to those who believe in him he has given his grace.

22. When Scripture says "He will reward every man according to his works" (Mt 16.27), do not imagine that works in themselves merit either hell or the kingdom. On the contrary, Christ rewards each man according to whether his works are done with faith or without faith in himself; and he is not a dealer bound by contract, but God our Creator and Redeemer.

23. We who have received baptism offer good works, not by way of repayment, but to preserve the purity given to us.

24. Every good work which we perform through our own natural powers causes us to refrain from the corresponding sin; but without grace it cannot contribute to our sanctification.

25. The self-controlled refrain from gluttony; those who have renounced possessions, from greed; the tranquil, from loquacity; the pure, from self-indulgence; the modest, from unchastity; the self-dependent, from avarice; the gentle, from agitation; the humble, from self-esteem; the obedient, from quarelling; the self-critical, from hypocrisy. Similarly, those who pray are protected from despair; the poor, from having many possessions; confessors of the faith, from the denial; martyrs, from idolatry. Do you see how every virtue that is performed even to the point of death is nothing other than refraining from sin? Now to refrain from sin is a work within our own natural powers, but not something that buys us the kingdom.

26. While man can scarcely keep what belongs to him by nature, Christ gives the grace of sonship through the Cross.

NOTES

[1] *On Galatians* 5,6, PG 61.673-4.

[2] E.g. see Saint Cyril of Jerusalem, *Catechetical Lectures* 4,2, PG 33.456B.

[3] *On First Thessalonians* 1, PG 62.394.

[4] 19, *Philokalia* 1, 126.

[5] Ibid. p. 127.

[6] "For salvation is not in the strength of man, nor in wisdom, but in the grace of God." Saint Basil, *Homilies on the Psalms* 33.2. PG 29.353C.

[7] E.g. see *Vorlesung üder den Römerbrief* (München, 1965), p. 142.

[8] Saint Gregory of Nyssa, *On Perfection*, in W. Jaeger (ed.), Gregorii Nysseni, *Opera*, vol. 8, 1 (Leiden, 1952), p. 213, PG 46.285B.

[9] *The Life in Christ*, trans. C. J. de Catanzaro (Crestwood, 1974), pp. 48-49.

[10] Ibid. p. 225.

[11] See *Von den guten Werken*, in WA 6.

[12] Council of Trent, Session 6, Canon 32. Denzinger-Schönmetzer (ed.), *Enchiridion Symbolorum Definitionum et Declarationum de rebus fidei et morum*, 36th ed. (Barcelona, 1976), p. 1582.

[13] *Homily* 33.7 *Erga* 10.338.

[14] Saint Maximos the Confessor, *Texts on Theology* 2.86, *Philokalia* 2, 159.

[15] Saint Gregory Palamas, *Dialogue of an Orthodox with a Baarlamite* 21, *Erga* 3, 298.

[16] Saint Nicholas Kabasilas, *The Life in Christ* 1.11, p. 63.

[17] See M. Weber, *The Protestant Ethic and the Spirit of Capitalism*, tr. Talcott Parsons (London, 1985), p. 114.

[18] See Saint Maximos Confessor, Texts on Love 2.8, *Philokalia* 2, 66. For other passages, see under "Self-love" in the Index.

[19] Saint John Chrysostom, *Commentary on John* 70.1, PG 59.383. *Commentary of Acts* 30.3, PG 60.225.

[20] *Texts on Love* 3.8, *Philokalia* 2,84.

[21] Saint Gregory of Nyssa, *On Perfection*, in W. Jaeger (ed.), Gregorii Nysseni, *Opera*, vol. 8, 1 (Leiden, 1952), p. 213, PG 46.285BC.

[22] Translation from the *Philokalia* 1, 126-27.

CHAPTER TWELVE

Combatting the Passions and Training in the Virtues

The subject of combatting the passions and training in the virtues occupies a central position in the teaching of the Fathers of the Church. This is natural, because this is the area where man's disposition to co-operate with the grace of God for his salvation and renewal is manifest in the most decisive way. In the pages which follow, it is not possible to present this important subject analytically. An attempt will, however, be put forward to trace its general lines and to note its most basic elements.

The passions and virtues express respectively man's life contrary to nature and in accord with nature. There is also, of course, the super-

113

natural life to which the supernatural passion of deification corresponds, which will occupy us at the end of this book.[1] But in order
for man to attain the supernatural passion of deification, he must
war against those passions of his which are contrary to his nature
and cultivate the life of the virtues which are in accord with his nature.

The passions are not sins; but the sinful conditions or diseases
of the soul which are given effect by sins. So, for example, vanity,
sensuality, enmity, evil desire, etc. are not sins, but passions while
to give them effect is to sin. It is possible, as Saint Dorotheos observes,
for someone to have passions, but to give them effect, that is, not
to reveal them in concrete sins.[2] Therefore, the commandments of
Christ look not only to combatting sins, but proceed also to uprooting
the passions. So, continues Saint Dorotheos, while the Law said, "Do
not commit adultery," Christ says, "nor desire it" (Ex 20.13 and Mt
5.27-8). And while the Law said, "Do not murder," Christ says, "nor
be angry" (Ex 20.15 and Mt 5.21-2). The purpose of the Law was
to teach us to do whatever we not wish to have happened to us. But
the purpose of Christ is to root our enmity itself, sensuality itself,
ambition itself and the other passions.[3]

The mother of the passions, according to patristic teaching, is
self-love, which is "a mindless love for the body."[4] Certainly there
is a good self-love which not only does not lead to the passions, but
also elevates man to the knowledge of God and perfection.[5] But the
self-love which co-incides with "the mindless love for the body" and
constitutes the mother of the passions turns man not only against
God but also against himself. Thus, the surprising phenomenon occurs that man becomes self-loving "against himself."[6] It happens,
that is, that he fights his own self in the name of love for himself.
This surprising phenomenon is due in the final analysis to ignorance,
or as Saint Maximos Confessor notes more precisely, to the "mindless
and senseless habit of ignorance, the mother of all evils."[7] Thus, the
prime cause of the passions, from which their mother, self-love, arises
is ignorance.

Man, as Saint Maximos observes, is led by abuse of his natural
powers into ignorance of the cause of his existence. "Thus, having
become a transgressor and ignorant of God," he subordinates the

intellectual potential of his soul to his senses. Thus, he continues, he is not only made similar to the mindless animals, but he even surpasses them in mindlessness, because he has transformed his reason, which was in accord with his nature, into one contrary to nature. As much, then, as he cared to know visible things only by his senses, so much was he tightly bound in his ignorance of God. As the iron grip of this ignorance tightened, so he tried to find support in the enjoyment of the material things which he knew. And the more he tried this enjoyment, the more he strengthened the intense longing (eros) of self-love which is born from it. Finally, the more he was concerned with the intense longing of self-love, so he contrived more ways to enjoy pleasure, which is simultaneously the offspring and goal of self-love.[8]

The submission of the intellectual potential of the soul to the senses characterizes the condition in which man finds himself after accepting the advice of the devil and withdrawing from God. This constitutes a general reversal of man's spiritual potentials, which leads to the general distortion of his existence. According to the tripart division of the soul into intellective, incensive, and appetitive aspects, the natural position of the intellective aspect is to govern and direct the two other parts, which together make up the possible aspect of the soul. Correspondingly, the incensive and appetitive aspects of the soul must be subordinated to the intellective aspect. When this does not happen, but the intellective — that is, the intellectual potential of the soul — is subordinated to the possible and serves it, then we have a condition of distortion. The passions enchain the intellect with material affairs and, like massive stones, they stand above it and keep it fixed to the earth, while it is by its nature lighter and swifter than fire.[9]

The intellect, which is the highest power of the soul, cannot be separated from it. The soul of man has many powers but is single. Therefore, when one of its powers is weakened, the whole of it is weakened: "The whole [soul] is weakened, therefore, when evil arises in any one of its powers, for they all share in that one [power] by virtue of the unity of the soul."[10] But since the passions start from the intellect of man (which is therefore characterized as the "first to suffer''), man cannot be delivered from them, if he does not cleanse his intellect. But even the subordination of the intellect to the passions does not occur except through the mediation of the senses, and especially the eyes. This is apparent with Eve herself, who first saw "that it was good to the sight, and beautiful to perceive, and then assenting in her heart, she touched and tasted of the forbidden tree."[11] Therefore, the cleansing must begin from the appetitive aspect of the soul. If this is not healed, the irascible agent cannot be healed. If these two are not healed, the intellect cannot be healed, that is, the intellective aspect of the soul.[12]

Man as a creature "in the image and likeness" of God can live and prove his existence worthwhile only in relation to and in communion with God. Whatever man is and whatever he has at his disposal, has meaning within the framework of this communion. All his powers and abilities exist in order to lead him to his archetype:

> We have received reason, in order to know Christ; desire in order to run to him. We possessed memory in order to bear him, since he was the archetype of those who have been created.[1]

Even what is at man's disposal exists "to make God known to man, to make man's life communion with God."[2] The world and the things of the world exist as signs of the presence of God and as causes of man's reference to his creator.

While the man should have his intellect fixed on God, should long for him and direct his steps toward him, he is instead ignorant of God, isolated in his self-love and enslaved to the tyranny of the passions. In order, then, for man to return to his natural condition, he ought to walk his opposite way. In other words, he ought to fight his passions, to conquer his self-love and know God. It is impossible for man to do this. However, God has made it possible by his incarnation in Christ. Christ who as perfect God reveals to man the God whom he does not know, and as perfect man carries fallen man back to his natural condition, opened the way for his salvation and renewal.

Whatever thought God offers to man by grace, man is called to live in his daily life. Here he engages in his struggle to combat the passions and to cultivate the virtues. In order to succeed, though, in this struggle of his, he needs above all to know the enemies which he has to confront and the targets which he must hit. Therefore, the Fathers of Church often indicated these enemies and spoke about the way to confront and combat them.

A schematic presentation of the evil thoughts was created by Evagrius Pontikos and it has been maintained in almost the entire later tradition. In his text, *Practical Treatise*, it is related that the most general thoughts, to which all the others are referred, are eight:

> First is that of gluttony and after that, of fornication; third, is avarice; fourth is dejection; fifth is wrath; sixth is listlessness; seventh is vanity; eighth is pride.[15]

In the subsequent text, each of these eight thoughts is analysed in the order in which it is listed. It is characteristic that Evagrios uses indifferently the word "thought" ("*logismos*" of gluttony, vanity), sometimes the name "demon" (of fornication, listlessness, pride), and sometimes the term "passion" (of avarice, dejection, wrath).

The thoughts are the means by which the demons fight monks. For those in the world, the demons use material things. Therefore, the warfare of monks is more difficult.[16] Certainly, all thoughts are not suggested by the demons, because even man's intellect is led to them.[17] The same principle must be accepted also in relation to the things which tempt those living in the world. In consequence, Evagrios presents a brief analysis of these thoughts, as well as the ways to confront them,[18] while he devotes a special essay to the same theme with the title, *On the Eighth Spirits of Wickedness*.[19] In this essay the same order is followed, except that wrath is placed before sorrow.

In the West, Saint John Cassian wrote on the same subject[20] following the order which we find in Evagrios' work *On the Eight Spirits of Wickedness,* while Saint Gregory the Great in his *Moralia,* besides some very few modifications which he made, replaces listlessness with envy (*invidia*) and limits the number of the eight spirits to seven, omitting pride. He saw pride as the mother of the passionate thoughts, as the eastern Fathers saw self-love.[21] But in the East, Saint John of Damascus retained the number eight in his work, also titled *On the Eight Spirits of Wickedness*,[22] as well as the order which we find in the text of the *Practical Treatise*. This order was supported chiefly by the monks' experience of spiritual struggles. In any case, the modifications which Saint Gregory the Dialogist made,[23] especially the replacement of listlessness by envy, were dictated by the special need for the spiritual edification of the faithful.

In the patristic literature, we can similarly confirm an interest in a general presentation of evil thoughts. From self-love, writes Saint Maximos Confessor, "are produced the three principal thoughts of desire: those of gluttony, avarice, and self-esteem."[24] As Evagrios Pontikos had already noted, these three thoughts correspond to those which the devil proposed to Christ. Firstly, he told Christ to make stones into bread, then to worship him in order to give him authority over the world; and finally, to jump from the highest part of the Temple, so that he might be glorified since he would suffer nothing. Further analysing the products of the three principal thoughts of desire which procede from self-love, Saint Maximos notes the following: "From the thought of gluttony is produced the thought of fornication; from the thought of avarice the thought of covetousness; and from the thought of vanity, the thought of pride.[25] Finally, from each of the three principle thoughts are produced the thoughts of wrath, dejection, remembrance of injuries, listlessness, envy, slander, etc.[26]

Saint Gregory Palamas follows a different order when he presents the three first or principal thoughts. At the beginning, he recalls avarice, which we justly called by the Apostle Paul, "the root of all evils" (1 Tim 6.10). In second place, he puts love of praise or vanity and in the third, gluttony.[27] Finally, referring to the products of these thoughts, he observes that from avarice are produced stinginess, speculation, plunder, and theft and that many other passions are nourished by it. From vanity springs pride, as well as envy, while from gluttony springs every fleshly impurity.

The passions as conditions contrary to nature distance man from virtue and lead him to vice. But vice is non-existent in itself. It has neither essence nor existence. The soul which is led into vice is punished by this, because it does not find a natural repose. Saint Dorotheos presents this position which is very widely known in the patristic tradition, noting the following characteristic examples.[28] Wood, when it has decayed a little, creates the worm. This worm, which did not exist before, but was created by the decomposition, eats the wood. The same happens with copper, which corrodes and consequently is destroyed by the rust. The same end comes to the cloth which is created by a moth and is ruined by one. So then, the soul creates evil, which was previously non-existent and insubstantial, and it is punished by it. Evil, then, as Saint Dorotheos summarizes it, "is sickness of the soul deprived of its own natural health, which is virtue.[29]

In order for man to remain on the path of virtue and not to deviate to right of left, he needs to be sober and to pay attention to himself. The Christian, then, is called to walk the royal road of moderation, as the Scripture urges: "Do not swerve to the right or the left, but travel on the royal road" (Prov 4.27 *LXX*. cf. Num 20.17).

In contrast with the passions which are combined with conditions contrary to nature, virtue corresponds to man's natural condition. As Maximos Confessor notes characteristically, "Thus, while we are in our present state we can actively accomplish the virtues by nature, since we have a natural capacity for accomplishing them."[30] This natural capacity of man to accomplish virtue proceeds from his natural relationship with God, in whose "image and likeness" he was created. This relationship is revealed and given effect by virtue. When, then, man is maintained in this position, he acts in accord with his nature and with virtue. Thus, Saint Athanasios the Great writes, "Do not fear when you hear of virtue, nor let this word seem strange to you, because it is found neither far from us nor outside of us, but is realized within us and is an easy matter. It is enough for us just to will it."[31] But the same thing does not happen when man abandons God. In this case, as we have said, he becomes absorbed in the world and isolated in his self-love. He does not refer himself to God in what he thinks and does, but turns to his own self. Therefore, he even considers his enslavement to his passions as natural.

As Origen rightly observed, man's soul is not "generative," but "receptive" of good things. It does not "generate" but "bears" virtues as a bride of Christ who is the only sower of good things.[32] Therefore, every kind of virtue, as Saint Gregory Palamas observes, "is produced in us when God acts in us," while when God is not active in us, "everything that proceeds from us is sin."[33]

The Fathers of the Church follow the biblical teaching, but they are also aware of the well-known comment of Aristotle that virtue constitutes a middle position between two evils, "the one by excess and the other by deficiency,"[34] and so they often characterize virtue as moderation. Thus for example, Saint Basil the Great writes: "For virtue is a certain moderation and proportion; excesses and deficiencies going beyond virtues both ways are a lack of symmetry and deformity." For instance, bravery is moderation, rashness is excess and cowardice is the deficiency.[35]

There is also in the Christian tradition the devision of virtues, known from the ancient Greek world, on the basis of a tripartite distinction of the soul. Thus, Evagrios Pontikos notes that the virtue of the intellective aspect is called "self-restraint and love and self-control," of the appetitive aspect, "courage and patience," while the virtue of the whole soul is "justice."[36] He continues by defining the special work of each virtue within the perspective of the Christian life, which he has in view. A little later, Saint Proklos, Patriarch of Constantinople, cites with some circumspection the four kinds of virtues of the ancient Greeks (moral judgment, self-restraint, courage, and justice) and advances the three Christian virtues of faith, hope and love.[37]

These three virtues, as Saint Proklos notes, are already presented by the Apostle Paul: "Now these three remain, faith, hope and love; and the greatest of these is love" (1 Cor 13.13; cf. 1 Th 1.3) Saint Ignatios of Antioch writes that faith is the beginning and love is the end. "And when these two are joined together in unity, it is God."[38] In fact, faith and love converge and are united between them. Faith mirrors love, which is God. And love confirms faith, which is self-abandonment to the love of God. Finally, hope is that power which joins man to God by transcending obstacles and overcoming the fickleness of time.[39]

In the final analysis, then, man's virtue is found in his return to God. When man cultivates faith, hope and love, he cultivates his bond with God and overcomes his self-love. Thus, while the passions are created by self-love and the abandonment or ignorance of God, the virtues are cultivated by love for God. In this case, even self-love is combatted, and it constitutes the mother of the passions, without this meaning that man's love for himself is also to be combatted. Self-love as "the unreasonable love for the body" is a false and distorted love. The true love of man for himself, the good self-love, contributes, as we have said, to his perfection.

Analyzing this, Saint Gregory Palamas observes the following: The faithful who love their souls and wish to guard them for eternal life, when they hear the threats and promises of God, are seized by fear of hell and endless suffering, and by a yearning for the kingdom of God and eternal bliss. Thus they are freed from their passions and hasten to be united with God, because he alone can deliver them from the suffering of hell and offer them eternal joy. In this way they acquire love for God; they are joined more with him and practice every kind of virtue.[40]

Saint Maximos the Confessor
A. Texts on Love (1.64-67)[41]

64. Some passions pertain to the body, others to the soul. The first are occasioned by the body, the second by external objects. Love self-control overcome both kinds, the first curbing the passions of the soul and the second those of the body.

65. Some passions pertain to the soul's incensive power, and others to its desiring aspect. Both kinds are aroused through the senses. They are aroused when the soul lacks love and self-control.

66. The passions of the soul's incensive power are more difficult to combat than those of its desiring aspect. Consequently our Lord has given a stronger remedy against them: the commandment of love.

67. While passions such as forgetfulness and ignorance affect but one of the soul's three aspects — the incensive, the desiring or the intelligent — listlessness alone seizes control of all the soul's powers ans rouses almost all the passions together. That is why this passion

is more serious than all the others. Hence our Lord has given us an excellent remedy against it, saying: "You will gain possession of your souls through your patient endurance" (Lk 21.19).

B. Various Texts on Theology, the Divine Economy, and Virtue and Vice 1.41-45[42]

41. Rebelling as we do against God through the passions and agreeing to pay tribute in the form of evil to that cunning tyrant and murderer of souls, the devil, we cannot be reconciled with God until we have first began to fight against the devil with all our strength. For even though we assume the name of faithful Christians, until we have made ourselves the devil's enemies and fight against him, we continue by deliberate choice to serve the shameful passions. And nothing of profit will come to us from our peace in the world, for our soul is in an evil state, rebelling against its own Maker and unwilling to be subject to his kingdom. It is still sold into bondage to hordes of savage masters, who urge it towards evil and treacherously contrive to make it choose the way which leads to destruction instead of that which brings salvation.

42. God made us so that we might become "partakers of the divine nature" (2 Pt 1.4) and sharers in his eternity, and so that we might come to be like him (cf. 1 Jn 3.2) through deification by grace. It is through deification that all things are reconstituted and achieve their permanence; and it is for its sake that which is not brought into being and given existence.

43. If we desire to belong to God in both name and reality, let us struggle not to betray the Logos to the passions, as Judas did (cf. Mt. 26.14-16), or to deny him as Peter did (cf. Mt 26.69-75). To deny the Logos is to fail through fear to do what is good; to betray him is deliberately to choose and commit sin.

44. The outcome of every affliction endured for the sake of virtue is joy, of every labour rest, and of every shameful treatment glory; in short, the outcome of all sufferings for the sake of virtue is to be

with God, to remain with him for ever and to enjoy eternal rest.

45. Because he wishes to unite us in nature and will with one another, and in his goodness urges all humanity towards this goal, God in his love entrusted his saving commandments to us, ordaining simply that we should show mercy and receive mercy (cf. Mt 5.7).

NOTES

[1]Chapter 16, "Deification," pp. 172-187.

[2]"For the passions are one thing, but sins are another... *Treatise* 1.6, ed. P.K. Chrestou (Thessalonike, 1981), p. 264; vol. 12 in the series *Philokalia of the Watchful and Ascetical Fathers.*

[3]Ibid. 1.9, p. 266-68.

[4]Saint Maximos Confessor, *Texts on Love* 3.57, *Philokalia* 2, 92.

[5]See Saint Maximos Confessor, *Various Texts* 1.32, p. 171; 1.50, p. 174; 5.97, p. 284, *Philokalia* 2. See also *To Thalassios*, PG 90.260CD.

[6]See Saint Maximos Confessor, *To Thalassios*, PG 90.257B.

[7]Ibid. PG 90.301B.

[8]Ibid. PG 90.253CD.

[9]Saint Maximos Confessor, *Texts on Love* 3,56, *Philokalia* 2,92.

[10]Saint Gregory Palamas, *Chapters on Prayer* 3, PG 150.1120C.

[11]Ibid. PG 150.1069B. Cf. Gen 3.6.

[12]Ibid. PG 150.1061A.

[13]Saint Nicholas Kabasilas, *The Life in Christ*, 6. PG 150.680A.

[14]A. Schmemann, *For the Life of the World* (Crestwood, 1973), p. 14.

[15]*Treastise* 6, A. Guillaumont et C. Guillaumont (éd.), Évagre le Pontique, *Traité pratique*, vol. 2, "Sources Chrétiennes" 171 (Paris, 1971), pp. 506-08.

[16]"The demons fight against those in the world through things, while against monks mostly through the thoughts, for they are deprived of things because of the desert. As it easier to sin in thought than in deed, so the warfare in the mind is more laborious than that constituted through things." Evagrios Pontikos, p. 608.

[17]For a more analytical treatment of the subject, see Evagrios Pontikos, *Texts of Discrimination* 2, *Philokalia* 1. 38-9.

[18]Ibid. 7-23, p. 42-52.

[19]PG 79.1145A-64D.

[20]*Sermon* 5, "On the Eight Vices," *Philokalia* 1, 73ff. PL 49.609D-642C.

[21]See further R. Gillet (ed.), Gregoire le Grand, *Morales sur Job*, livres 1 et 2, "Sources Chrétiennes" 32 (Paris, 1950), p. 89 ff. Cf. also Th. Spidlik, *La spiritualité de l' Orient Chrétien* (Rome, 1978), p. 246.

[22]PG 95.79A-86B.

[23]I.e. Saint Gregory the Great, called the "Dialogist" from his *Dialogues* which were highly regarded in the East—tr.

[24]*Texts on Love* 3.56, *Philokalia* 2, 92.

[25]It must be noted here that vanity and pride present themselves to monks and laity with different marks. Thus, in monks they are conjoined with virtue and its achievements while in those in the world with beauty, wealth, power, and moral judgement. See Saint Maximos Confessor, *Texts on Love* 3.84, *Philokalia* 2, 96. Cf. Saint Gregory Palamas, *To Xenia*, PG 150.1065A.

[26]Saint Maximos Confessor, *Texts on Love* 3.56, *Philokalia* 2, 92; Cf. Saint Thalassios the Libyan, *On Love, Self-Control, and Life in accordance with the Intellect* 3.88-90, *Philokalia* 2,224.

[27]*To Xenia*, PG 150.1061A-69A. See further, G.I. Mantzarides, *The Deification of Man*, tr. Liadain Sherrard (Crestwood, 1984), p. 80 ff.

[28]*Treatise* 10.6, ed. P. K. Chrestou (Thessalonike, 1981), p. 456, vol. 12 in the series *Philokalia of the Watchful and Ascetical Fathers.*

[29]Ibid.

[30]*Various Texts* 1,75, *Philokalia* 2, 181.

[31]*Life of Saint Anthony* 20, PG 26.873A.

[32]"Besides, then, as it is natural to the way of woman to give birth, so (the soul) is able to bear practical and intellectual virtues." *On John.* frag. 45.

[33]*Sermon* 33.7, *Erga*, 10,338.

[34]*Ethica Nicomachea* 2.9.1109a.

[35]*On Isaiah* 5.174, PG 30.409C; Cf. Saint Gregory of Nyssa, *Song of Songs* 9, tr C. McGambley (Boston, 1987), p. 180 and D. Tsamis, "The Teaching of Gregory the Theologian on Moderation," *Kleronomia* 1 (1969), 275 ff, in Greek.

[36]*Traité pratique*, 89, pp. 680-82.

[37]*Letter to the Armenians on Faith* 1-3, PG 65.856C-7D.

[38]*To the Ephesians* 14.1.

[39]"For hope, transcending the obstacles in its way, unites what desires to the beloved, overcoming the flow of time in relation to the future. And love is the culmination of God's hidden purpose for us, for it persuaded God the Word, who is always present on earth, to come in the flesh. Thus each concurs with the others: for faith is the mirror of love, and love is the confirmation of faith." Saint Proklos of Constantinople, *Letter to the Armenians on Faith* 3, PG 65.857CD.

[40]*Homily* 33.6-7, *Erga* 11, p. 338.

[41]Translation from the *Philokalia* 2, 59-60.

[42]Translation from the *Philokalia* 2,172-3.

CHAPTER THIRTEEN

Mental Prayer

The *Sober Contemplation*, the work of an anonymous monk of the Holy Mountain written last century, begins with the following sentences:

> Our Lord Jesus Christ says in his divine and holy Gospel, "He who believes in me, from his belly shall flow rivers of living water." Whoever, then, wishes this living water of the Holy Spirit to pour forth from his heart as if from some perpetual spring, let him struggle to acquire in his heart mental and heartfelt prayer, that is "Lord Jesus Christ, Son of God, have mercy on me."[1]

This mental and heart-centered prayer, which consists essentially in the invocation of the name of Jesus, is also called the prayer of Jesus or the Jesus Prayer. This invocation in the final analysis goes back to the time of Jesus himself. It is related in the Holy Gospels, when the blind man of Jericho was informed of the passage of Jesus, he began to cry, "Jesus, Son of David, have mercy on me" (LK 18.38; Mk 10.48). It was not difficult for this invocation to be adapted appropriately and used as a Christian prayer. Exactly when this happened is not known. But nevertheless, at least by the middle of the sixth century, we have mention of the use of the prayer of Jesus in its present form.[2]

This prayer is also called the "monologist" prayer, because it is contained in only one phrase. Since this phrase, by which the faithful invokes the mercy of Christ, is also related to the phrase of the tax-collector in the well-known gospel parable (Lk 18.13), it is also called the prayer of the tax-collector. Finally, the names "mental" and "prayer of the heart" originate respectively from the mind and the heart of man where the prayer is accomplished.

The practice of the prayer of Jesus begins with the audible repetition of the phrase, "Lord Jesus Christ, Son of God, have mercy on me," which can be expanded or abbreviated. The abbreviation usually occurs by limiting it to the words, "Lord Jesus, have mercy on me" or "Lord Jesus," while it is expanded by adding the words, "the sinner," whence we have the phrase, "Lord Jesus Christ, Son of God, have mercy on me, the sinner." The limitation of the prayer to a few words is thought necessary to maintain concentration in one's self and one's uninterrupted attachment to God.

This prayer with its constant repetition and with help of God is tranferred step by step fom man's lips to his mind. It can even cease to be repeated audibly and can be performed with the mind alone. The mental performance of the prayer must not be considered as an intellectual matter, but as a manifestation of the whole human existence. Further, the goal of the prayer is that the mind descend to the heart which, in the characteristic formulation of Saint Gregory Palamas, constitutes "the primary intellective organ of the flesh."[3] The Christian finds there the seal of Christ and the gift of holy Baptism.[4]

As Saint John of Sinai (Klimakos) writes, the invocation of the name of Jesus constitutes the principal weapon of the faithful in their struggle against evil: "Scourge your enemies with the name of Jesus, for there is no weapon in heaven or on earth."⁵ With this prayer, temptations are confronted and the passions engaged in battle. When this prayer takes root in the heart, the passions are uprooted from it and man become really free. "Because, if it happens that mental prayer does not dwell in that place from which the passions gush forth, these passions are not being cut off."⁶

Mental prayer, according to the orthodox tradition, is taught to the monk or the faithful by his elder. But in exceptional cases, one proceeds by himself with humility and invoking the grace of God. The presuppositions for its discipline are fasting, vigil, hardships, and great humility. But all these remain just struggles, without the grace of God. But when the grace of God comes, this prayer takes root in one's heart and communion with God is maintained ceaselessly. Further, and more generally, without the grace of the Holy Spirit, every human virtue remains dead and ineffectual.

> For only when [the Holy Spirit] comes and dwells in us, does he join our dead virtuous deeds — like lifeless members broken apart from each other — by sinews of spiritual strength. He unites them with love for God, and then proves us to be young from the old and living from the dead; the soul cannot live otherwise.⁷

The practice of mental prayer was combined by the hesychast monks of Byzantium with an adaption of a psycho-somatic method of self-concentration. According to this method, the monk sits with his chin supported on his chest and his gaze turned toward his navel, repeating continuously the prayer of Jesus, and combining it with the rhythm of his breath. At the same time, he tries to detach his mind from every distraction and to concentrate it in words of the prayer. By frequent repetition and intense attention, the prayer is transferred from the mind to the heart of man. Thus, the whole human existence prays and lives the prayer.

Barlaam the Calabrian, the enemy of the hesychasts, thought that Nikephoros the Athonite had introduced this method during the fourteenth century. In opposition, the champion of the hesychasts, Saint Gregory Palamas, maintained that Nikephoros was in continuity with a more ancient patristic tradition.⁸ The most important texts in which the method of prayer is described are *On Sobriety and Guarding the Heart* by Nikephoros, and the *Method of Holy Attention and Prayer* which was attributed to Saint Symeon the New Theologian, but is in fact a text of the twelfth century.[9] It is self-evident, certainly, that this method does not form a constitutive element of the prayer, but simply a means for self-concentration and the "uniform introversion" of the mind.[10]

Saint Gregory Palamas says that this prayer becomes possible for man, when he accepts within him the gift of prayer. This gift, which is offered by God to those who persist in prayer with humility and discipline, remains unceasingly within them:

> For, since they have become participants in the perpetually moving and tireless grace, they have the prayer rooted in their souls and ceaselessly acting, in accord with the one who said, "I sleep but my heart keeps watch."[11]

Thus, uninterrupted prayer does not form the activity of a single day for man, but the fruit of his co-operation with the grace of the Holy Spirit which visits him and acts mystically within him.

When a contemporary monk of the Holy Mountain was once asked how it is possible for someone to work or to talk and still to pray, he answered quite naturally: If now, while we are speaking together, I listen to my heart, it will be saying, "Lord Jesus Christ, have mercy on me." Of course, not all monks reach this level. Many struggle and some are lazy. But there are not those who live constantly with the prayer. In spite of the secularization which dominates in our time, there are still some today to maintain ceaselessly man's communication with God.

Finally, mental prayer is not practiced only by the monks, but also by a number of the faithful who live in the world. Indeed, especially in recent years with the spread of patristic texts and the return to the sources of Orthodox spiritual life, mental prayer is becoming more and more dear to the faithful who live in the world. The constantly increasing communication of secular Christians with Hagioritic (i.e. of the Holy Mountain, Mt Athos) or other contributes greatly to this. These monks as spiritual fathers or counsellors influence their spiritual lives and direct them in mental prayer.

Thus, the faithful are on the way to realizing the injunction of the Apostle Paul to "pray without ceasing" (1 Thes 5.17), an injunction which is not addressed only to monks or to some special category of the faithful, but to all Christians.

Saint Symeon of Thessalonike On Holy Prayer[12]
What the Holy Prayer Is.

This sacred prayer, then, the invocation of our Savior, "Lord Jesus Christ, Son of God, have mercy on me," is a prayer, and a blessing, and a confession of faith. It is productive of the Holy Spirit, a dispenser of divine gifts, a purifying of the heart, a chasing away of demons, a dwelling of Jesus Christ, a source of spiritual thoughts and reflections. It is for the forgiveness of sins, an infirmary of bodies, a dispenser of divine enlightenment, a fountain of God's mercy, a distributor of revelations and divine initiation in humility, and the only salvation. For even salvation bears in itself the name of our God, which is the only name invoked on us, that of Jesus Christ the Son of God; and our salvation is in nothing else, as the Apostle says (Acts 4.12).

And so, it is a prayer, because in it we seek divine mercy; and a blessing, because we give ourselves to Christ through his intercession. It is a confession, because Peter was blessed when he made this confession; and it is productive of the Spirit, because "no one can say 'Lord Jesus' except in the Holy Spirit" (1 Cor 12.3). It is a dispenser of divine gifts because, as Christ says to Peter, "for this (his confession of faith) I will give you the keys of the kingdom of heaven" (Mt 16.19). It is a purification of the heart because he sees God who calls and cleanses the one who sees. It chases away demons because in the name of Jesus Christ all demons were and are expelled. It is a dwelling of Christ because in our recollection of him, Christ is in us and through recollection he dwells in us, filling us with gladness, for "I remembered," it says, "the Lord and was made glad"

(Ps 76.4 *LXX*).

It is the source of spiritual thoughts and reflections because Christ is the treasury of all wisdom and knowledge which he grants to those in whom he dwells. It is a redemption for our sins since through this "whatever you shall loose," it says "shall be loosed in heaven" (Mt 16.19). It is the infirmary of souls and bodies because "in the name of Jesus Christ, rise and walk" (Acts 3.6), it says; and "Aeneas, Jesus Christ heals you" (Acts 9.34). It is a dispenser of divine enlightenment because Christ is the true light and he transmits his splendor and grace to those who call upon him. "May the splendor of the Lord our God be upon us" (Ps 89.17 LXX), it says, and "whoever follows me shall have the light of life" (Jn 8.12).

It is a fountain of divine mercy because we ask for mercy and the Lord is merciful and has compassion on all who call upon him; he avenges quickly those who cry to him. It is a distributor of revelations and divine initiation to the humble because this was given to the fisherman, Peter, through a revelation of the Father in heaven. Likewise Paul was carried away in Christ and heard revelations, and Christ always effects this. It is the only salvation because our salvation is in no one else, says the Apostle (Acts 4,42), and "this Christ is the savior of the world" (Jn 4.42). Therefore it shall still be on the last day, that "every tongue shall confess' and sing in praise willingly or unwillingly, "that Christ is Lord, to the glory of God the Father" (Phil 2.11).

This is the sign of our faith since we are called Christians, and the testimony that we are from God. "For every spirit that confesses that the Lord Jesus Christ has come in flesh is from God," it says, as we have said before, and what does not confess is not from God (1 Jn 4.3). This belongs to the Antichrist who does not confess Jesus Christ.

Therefore it is necessary that all the faithful without ceasing confess this name, both for the proclamation of faith and for love of our Lord Jesus Christ, from whom nothing must ever separate us at all, for the grace which comes from his name, for the forgiveness and remission and healing, for blessing and enlightenment and above all for salvation.

For in this holy name the apostles worked miraculously and taught. And the holy Evangelist says, "These things have been written so that you may believe that Jesus is the Christ, the Son of God" (Jn 20.31) — here is faith! — and so that believing you may have life in his name" (Jn 20.31) — and here is salvation and life!

NOTES

[1] Thessalonike 1979, p. 17 in Greek.

[2] See further A Monk of the Eastern Church (Archimandrite Lev Gillet), *The Jesus Prayer*, Crestwood, NY, 1987; B. Schultze, "Untersuchungen über des Jesus-Gebet," *Orientalia Christiana Periodica* 18 (1952) 319-43; Kallistos Ware (Bp. of Diokleia), *The Power of the Name* 2nd ed., Oxford 1986.

[3] *Triads in Defence of the Holy Hesychasts* 2.2.27, *Erga* 2, p. 402.

[4] See Gregory of Sinai, *Acrostich Chapters* 113, PG 150.1277D.

[5] *The Ladder* 21, PG 88.945C.

[6] *Sober Contemplation*, p. 35.

[7] Saint Symeon the New Theologian, *Ethical Treatises* 7,327-332, J. Darrouzes, (ed.), *Traités théologiques et éthiques*, "Sources Chrétiennes" 129, Paris 1967, p. 178.

[8] *Triads in Defence of the Holy Hesychasts* 1.2.12, *Erga* 2, p. 142.

[9] See Hausherr, "La méthode d' oraison hésychaste," *Orientalia Christiana* 9,2 no. 36, Rome 1927, and "Note sur l'inventeur de la méthode d' oraison hésychaste," *Orientalia Christiana* 20, no. 66, Rome 1930, pp. 179-82. H. G. Beck, *Kirche und theologische Literatur im Byzantinischen Reich*, Munichen 1959, pp. 586 and 693.

[10] Cf. Ps. Dionysios the Areopagite, *On the Divine Names* 4.9, PG 3.705A.

[11] *Triads in Defence of the Holy Hesychasts*, 2.1.31, *Erga* 2, 318 citing the Song of Solomon 5.2.

[12] Chap. 96, PG 155.544D-48C.

CHAPTER FOURTEEN

Social Action and
the Eschatological Perspective

Man, as a social being, lives and acts socially, that is, he lives and acts in a personal relationship and communion with his fellow men. This phenomenon creates social life. But the whole of the formal and impersonal relationships of men are also characterized as social life, relationships which often not only do not express his spontaneous personal sociability, but alter it and distort it. This second form of social life appears in our time so overdeveloped that it literally threatens the whole of human social life. Thus, in everyday social relationships and expressions, but even beyond these, there unfolds a barely perceptible but, at the same time all-powerful mesh of ob-

132

jectified social relationships and institutions which literally chain social life and drain its vital sap.

This altered form of social life unfolds together with an altered form of social activity. The well-known German sociologist, Max Weber, distinguished four types of socials activity analogous to the motives which drive man to it: a) expedient, b) evaluative, c) emotional, and d) traditional. In contemporary society, the first form of social activity has developed so much that it tends to make the following three disappear. Expediency in personal and social life has become so over-grown that it pushes aside evaluative and emotional motives and criteria. Furthermore, the connection with the past is weakening and its relationship with the present has become superficial.

Still, with contemporary social systems, the collectivity or the individuality of man is one-sidedly emphasized. But collectivity and individuality are abstract concepts which do not express the reality of individual and social life. Man's collectivity exists as an expression of his life as a person. His individuality exists in relation to his life in society. Communion does not exist independently of concrete persons, or a person independently of a concrete society. Therefore, not even man's social activity can be considered independently of his life in society. When these truths are abandoned, the person is crushed and the natural of social life and activity is alienated. The maintenance of the dialectical relationship of persons and society which constitutes the sole condition for the correct development of personal and social life and activity becomes a shell or is even abandonned.

In the face of such an alienation of social activity and life, the testimony of Christian truth becomes literally imperative.

The Orthodox Church always puts the person before any impersonal or objective reality or value whatsoever. This becomes obvious in her dogmatic teaching and in her positions on man's ethical and social life.

But the truth itself, according to biblical and patristic teaching, is personal. Christ is the truth (Jn 1.6), and the truth in the personal and social life of men is experienced in its fulness only as a personal sharing and communion in the truth of Christ. This truth is not found outside of men's life in society, but is revealed within it. Life in society is of the highest value: "Behold how good it is and how pleasant for brothers to dwell together. For in this, the Lord has promised eternal life."[1] The fraternal society of man in itself, beyond every expediency or usefulness, beyond every gift or productivity, is the "good" and the pleasant" which is extolled by the hymn. It is this which gives man value as a creature in the image of the Triadic God, and which finds its absolute fulness in the kingdom of God.

On the other hand, one cannot ignore the enormous difficulties entailed by maintaining the priority of the person within social life, perhaps especially in our time. Social life is dominated by powers which overwhelm man and his freedom. Man's place in contemporary industrial and post-industrial society is becoming more and more impersonal and anonymous. Mutual understanding, compassion, mutual support, and partnership are all disappearing. The particularity of the person is pushed aside. His place in society is identified with the role which he exercises.

> Within the role which he plays, beneath the mask he wears, man remains always alone . . . Loneliness cannot be overcome within society, within the mass of man, in an objectified world.[2]

Only when one acquires a certain distance from the world and from the structures which have been formed within him, can he sees it more accurately and not become its slave. An asceticism within the world which maintains the individual's self-assurance is irreconcilable with the spirit of Christian love. Since Christians who live in the world can easily be pushed in this direction, the existence of monasticism is necessary.

Orthodox monasticism with its communal spirit — a spirit which always formed the ideal of life the faithful within the world — has kept alive up to the present the ascetical spirit of Christianity. One sees this today on the Holy Mountain. A very good acquaitance with it and approach to it are not only interesting, but also revelatory of social life, and so the solution of many problems in contemporary society are to be found there.

The characteristic mark of the life of Orthodox monastics is the eschatological perspective. Still more generally, the spiritual experience is lived and expressed in an eschatological perspective. And further, the supreme spiritual nourishment of the faithful, the Sacrament of the Holy Eucharist, clearly has an eschatological character. It is the mystery of the presence of God among men and the assumption of men into the kingdom of God. The faithful, when they share in this sacrament, share in the communion of the future age. They are united with their God and Father, near whom they find all their brothers as well. So, while they live and move within the world, they feel themselves to be citizens of the kingdom of God.

The Christian life has a transcendent perspective. It is a life which "originates in this life and arises from it. It is perfected, however, in the life to come, when we shall have reached that last day."[3] This perspective, which is founded in the sacrament of the Holy Eucharist, has a catalytic importance for the personal and social life of the faithful in the world. Within this perspective, the world and the things of the world are put in a special light.

The phrase of Christ, "without me you can do nothing" (Jn 15.5), is not just a figure of speech. It is not hard to understand this truth in its final results, if one includes the instability of time and contemplates the final and decisive measure, which is death. Death frustrates man and everything human. Conversely, Christ, who is "the resurrection and the life" (Jn 11.25) for man, is the only value for anything human. Thus, no human expression at all can find true value without this transcendent perspective.

Man is accustomed to build his life from the self-evident perspective of his own preservation. But when death, which inevitably constitutes life's final word, is included in the perspective of human life, everything that precedes it is contradicted. And so, everything which cannot withstand the test of death is, finally, futile. So, for example, a unidimensional economic, social, moral, or any other kind of success, which is not included in the broadest perspective of man's overall worth, is finally futile. Conversely, an economic, social, moral, or any other kind of failure which does serve in his overall worth has a broader positive sense.

Man usually limits his perspective to secular immediacy and considers the world and the things of this world as absolute values. In this way though, he is unjust to himself and creates insoluble problems in his personal and social life. The world is too small to satisfy man. Indeed, human desire is infinite and unlimited. Only by transcending the things of this world can man's infinite desire be satisfied. Only with such a transcendence can the solution to the age-old problems which torment his existence be found.

Within the eschatological perspective, the different problems of man's personal and social life are relativized and considered in their conventional dimensions. This relativization constitutes as well the best assumption for correctly confronting and solving them. In fact, when these problems are considered in themselves, they are magnified excessively in man's eyes and crush them. And so, the attempts to confront and solve them are, naturally, spasmodic and create new problems. Conversely, their relativization within the eschatological perspective gives the Archimedean position to confront them.[4]

Even the greatest oppositions are abolished by the eschatological perspective, which is summed up in the last analysis between life and death. Death is not the end of life. Life is not the nurse of death. The present life is but the beginning of the future one. And the future life is what gives worth to the present one. The crucifixion does not prevent giving life; and giving life does not bypass the crucifixion. In the Orthodox Church, Good Friday and Easter Sunday constitute a single and indivisible unity. On Good Friday, the day of Christ's sacrifice, the Holy Eucharist is not celebrated. Conversely, Easter Sunday, the day of the resurrection, is celebrated by the offering of the bloodless sacrifice.

This perspective, which has sealed the history of the orthodox peoples, is maintained up to the present. The spirit in which life is viewed, the way in which death is confronted, the attitude which governs daily behavior, the disposition which characterizes the various expressions still testify to its influence. It is not necessary to visit the Holy Mountain or the various other monasteries of the Orthodox Church to ascertain the existence of this eschatological perspective. Even within the world, especially of course, in the rural areas with simple people, one can easily distinguish traces of this perspective.

Without ignoring the importance of the various historical and social factors which have influenced the traditional orthodox people and which again are not unrelated to their religious tradition, one cannot fail to distinguish the features of this eschatological perspective. Thus, one sees in these people that life is not cut off from death. The sense of the futility of the world remains alive. Silence about death has not yet been imposed. The meaning of life is not exhausted in labor and production. Not even the concentration of capital has social self-assurance as a goal nor is it combined with a worldly discipline, as in the countries of the West, but with an enjoyment and relaxation within the world, or with philanthropy and charity which respectively reveal the sense of the futility of the world or the renunciation of its goods for another reality.

Certainly, all these elements were much more intense in the past. If one reads the byzantine writers or studies the history of the orthodox peoples during the time of Turkish rule, he will see how alive the eschatological orientation of the faithful was. One gains almost the same sense when one reads the texts of Dostoyevsky, Makriyannis or Papadiamantis. But secularization, which has spread even in the traditionally orthodox territories with technological civilization as its tool, has inaugurated a new condition.[5] It is opposed to the eschatological perspective of Orthodoxy and limits man to immediacy. Within this climate, there has appeared a secularized eschatology as a substitute for religious eschatology. It has been dissociated from God and the love of God for man and is considered anthropocentric. In place of the kingdom of God or of paradise is put the kingdom of man or some terrestrial paradise to which man hopes to attain with his science and technology — if he is finally able to avoid a massive catastrophe by using his conquests for his benefit.

Saint Kosmas Aitolos:
Teaching A1 (Extract)[6]

It is natural for us to love our brothers because we are of one

nature; we have one baptism, one faith; we receive the holy
Sacraments; we hope to enjoy one paradise.

The man is fortunate indeed who has been found worthy to receive
these two loves in his heart; love for God and love for his brothers.
He possesses all that is good and cannot commit sin. Whoever does
not have God in his heart has the devil. Whoever has the devil
possesses all that is evil and commits every kind of sin.

Suppose we do thousands and thousands of good deeds, my
brothers, fasts, prayers, almsgiving, and we pour out our blood for
love of our Christ, but it perhaps we do not have both these loves,
but have hatred and enmity for our brothers, all these good deeds
that we have done are of the devil and we shall go to hell.

But, you want to say, because of that little enmity which we have
for our brothers, while we have done so many good deeds, will we
really go to hell? Yes, my brothers, we shall go because of that, because
that enmity is a poison of the devil. We put a little yeast into a hun-
dred kilos of flour and it has so much strength that it can make that
much dough rise. Enmity is just like that. It turns all those good deeds
that we have done and makes them all poison of the devil.

Dear Christians, how are you getting along here? Do you have
love for each other? If you want to be saved, don't seek any other
thing in this world except love.

Is there anyone among you kind folks who loves his brothers? Let
him stand up and speak to me that I may bless him and have all Christians forgive him, that he might receive a forgiveness which he could
not find if he gave a thousand bags of money.

"Saint of God, I love God and I love my brothers, teacher."

Good, my child. Receive my blessing. What is your name?"

"Kostas."

"What is your trade?"

"I'm a shepherd. I tend sheep."

"The cheese that you sell, do you weigh it?"

"Yes, I do."

"You, my child, have learned to weigh cheese and I have learned
to weigh love. Is the scale ashamed of its owner?"

"No."

"Now I will weigh your love and, if it is true and not short, then I will bless you and I will have all Christians forgive you. How can I understand you, my child? How do you love your brothers? Now, I who walk about and teach in the world, I say that I love Kostas like my own eyes. You hear me now saying that I love you, but you don't believe it. You want to test me first and then you will believe me."

"I have a loaf of bread to eat, but you do not. If then I give you a piece, since you don't have any, then I am showing that I love you. But if I should eat the whole loaf and you were to go hungry, what would I be showing? I would show that the love which I have for you is false. I have two glasses of wine to drink; you have none. If then I give you some of it to drink, then I show that I love you. But if, though, I do not give you any, the love is counterfeit. I have two or three shirts; you have none and are cold. If then I take one off and give it to you, then the love is true. But if I should have shirts kept in a chest to be eaten by worms while you go about bare, it is a counterfeit love."

"You are sad. Your mother has died, or your father, or your child, or you are sick. If then I come to console you, then my love is true. If, though, you are in tears and grieving while I sit and eat, drink, sing, and am merry, my love is false."

"Do you love that poor child?"

"I do."

"If you loved him, you would take him a little shirt, because he is bare, and he would pray for your soul. Then your love would be true; while now it is counterfeit. Isn't it counterfeit, dear Christians? We don't fill our granary with a torch, nor do we enter paradise with false love."

"Now do as you wish, my child, to make your love golden. Take and clothe a lot of poor children, and then I will have them forgive you. Will you do it?"

"I will."

"Dear Christians, Kostas understands that the love which he has for his brothers until now was false and he wants to turn it to gold, to clothe the poor children. Since we have taught him and made him blush a bit. I ask you to say for Mr Kostas three times, 'May God forgive you and have mercy on you.''

NOTES

[1]Anavathmoi, plagal 4th tone, antiphon 4, 1st troparion.

[2]Tr. from the Greek version of N. Berdiaeff, *Five Reflections on Existence*, see Triantaphyllou and S. Gounelas (Athens, 1983), p. 191.

[3]Saint Nicholas Kabasilas, *The New Life in Christ*, p. 43.

[4]Archimedes said, "Give me a lever long enough and a place to stand and I can move the world"—tr.

[5]See further G.I. Mantzaridis, *Sociology of Christianity* (Thessalonike, 1990), p. 137, in Greek.

[6]Cf. Nomikos M. Vaporis, *Father Kosmas: The Apostle of the Poor* (Brookline, 1977), p. 20 ff.

CHAPTER FIFTEEN

Truth and Freedom

The manifestation of the Holy Spirit in the world is the manifestation of truth and freedom. The Holy Spirit is "the Spirit of truth" (Jn 14.17, 15.26, 16,13) and the breath of the Holy Spirit is the breath of freedom (v. 2 Cor 3.17).

Knowledge of the truth has always been a very deep human desire. However, what man has found and is finding is that, in spite of all his efforts, he has not succeeded in discovering absolute truth. It is natural for this discovery to weary him to lead him to disillusionment, not only about the possibility of finding it, but even about its existence. The question that Pilate addressed to Christ is characteristic on this point: "What is truth?" (Jn 18.38)

This question, as become obvious in its context, does not express a desire to discover the truth, but pure scepticism and the final indifference to the truth by a man who has become reconciled to conventionalism and the vanity of the world. Pilate is interested in solving the practical problems which he confronts. The essence of truth does not seem to occupy him especially.

But this same problem is formulated as an agonizing question by many who really do desire the truth. It is quite natural to wonder: What is truth, then? How can someone know it and live it?

The Church's answer to this question is clear. Truth is not some abstract idea, so that man can reflect on it or understand it. Nor again is it some concrete object for him to study or acquire. Truth is a person. It is Christ. Christ himself said, "I am truth" (Jn 13.16).

To identify truth with Christ means though, by an elementary logical principle, the denial of its identification with anything else other than Christ. That is, if Christ is the truth, then whatever is not Christ or has no relationship with Christ cannot be the truth or have a relationship with the truth. Again, if there is a truth independent of Christ, then either Christ is not the truth or the truth of Christ is not the whole truth.

Man is accustomed to identifying truth with the data of his senses. This is his original sin. But the truth in its existential fulness transcends the senses: it is the source and fulness of life. Its identification with sensible things is due to man's submission to decay and death. But this truth is falsified and dies with man. Only by the transcendence of sense data the truth's connection with life become possible. This is realized in the resurrection of Christ.

Of course, there exists in the world a multitude of ephemeral truths which man approaches either with science or art or in some other manner. But even these are not unrelated to Christ who, as the eternal Word of God, is the one "though whom" and "for whom all things were created" (Col 1.16).

The truth we are talking about here and from which every partial truth draws its sense and content is not limited to immediacy, but refers to the nature of the existence of the world and of man. According to Christian teaching, then, this truth is found only in Christ who is the eternal Word of God.

This truth enters into the world with Christ and becomes accessible to man by the grace of the Holy Spirit. Christ, as perfect God and perfect man, incarnates and reveals the real truth to the world. The Holy Spirit, as the Spirit of truth, offers each of us severally the truth which Christ manifests to the world. Christ as truth does not come to satisfy man's curiosity for knowledge, but to reveal the true sense and purpose of his existence to him. Christ, who is the truth, is at the same time life as well. Finally, Christ is also the way which man is called to walk in order to know the truth and conquer death..

Death, the abolisher of human existence, finally leads man to destruction and oblivion, while conversely the life of Christ which conquers death recalls man from oblivion and ruin. This recalling of man is realized by his assumption into the truth of Christ. This direct relationship of life with truth is expressed in the Church's literature by the use of those words as synonyms. So, for example, Saint Ignatios of Antioch characterizes those who deny Christ as advocates "of death rather than of truth."[1] Here it is not life that is presented as the opposite of death, but truth. Thus, truth stands in the place of life is identified with it.

When man shares by the grace of the Holy Spirit in the truth of Christ, he finds true freedom: "You shall know the truth and the truth shall free you" (Jn 8.32). Real freedom is a fruit of the truth which is identified with true life. Freedom is not a deprivation, but fulness. Man, by the grace of the Holy Spirit, ceases to be a mortal and transitory existence and becomes a participant in the immortal life of Christ. The grace of the Holy Spirit with the Sacraments of the Church frees man from the earthly root of Adam and grafts him onto the spiritual root of Christ who, as victor over death and source of life, offers true life and liberation from the bonds of death. When man is limited by decay and death, it is to be expected that he will feel and live like a slave. But when he is redeemed from these bonds, he acquires the conditions for true freedom.

The locus of true freedom is the Church. This is so because the Church is the place where the activity of the Holy Spirit is manifest: "Where the Spirit of the Lord is, there is freedom" (2 Cor 3.17). The freedom of the Holy Spirit in the Church replaces the slavery of the Law which reigned in the old Israel. Incorrubtibility and life succeed the inner law of decay and death. Thus the Church constitutes the spiritual locals of renewal and the perfection of men as children of God within the truth of Christ and the freedom of the Holy Spirit.

With the Church, Christianity has come essentially to answer the basic problem of human freedom. If we take away freedom, the work of the divine economy ceases to have any meaning — the Law and the prophets, the incarnation of the Word of God, his death and resurrection, the descent of the Holy Spirit and finally the establishment of the Church. Freedom is the atmosphere within which truth moves. And so truth does not exist where freedom does not exist.

God did not want to deprive man of freedom. He became himself man and was crucified for man. He did not want to relieve man of the weight of his freedom, and therefore he accepted the weight of the cross. Thus man is saved while he remains man, that is, free because, in reality, man does not exist without freedom:

> For, remove our free will and we will not be the image of God, nor a reasonable and intellectual soul. Our nature will be corrupted in us, since it will not be what it was necessary for it to be.[2]

In spite of all this, the spirit of slavery and servility often dominates in the consciousness of the members of the Church and sufficatingly limits the freedom of the Holy Spirit. In the name of order, in the name of agreement, in the name of obedience and discipline, conditions are often created which alienate the ecclesial community and choke its charismatic character. But on the other hand, in the name of freedom, in the name of tolerance, in the name of personal particularity and of charismatic variety, tensions are formed which explode the ecclesial unity and dissolve the charismatic community. The harmonious synthesis of order and freedom, of agreement and toleration, of obedience and personal particularity, of discipline and charismatic variety is a subtle matter which can exist only in the climate of Christian love. Furthermore, freedom, like the truth which leads to freedom, cannot be understood in the Church independently of love. The love of God which was revealed in Christ offers man truth and freedom; and the only atmosphere in which man can maintain truth and freedom is the atmosphere of love.

Even truth and freedom demand accountability and entail risks. When man prefers irresponsibility and certainty, he avoids truth and freedom. Therefore, instead of living by the truth of Christ and the freedom of the breath of the Holy Spirit, he is handed over to the deceit of the world and to the slavery of the legalistic mentality. Instead of perceiving the Church as a source of truth and freedom, he sees it as an institution of morbid conservatism and ritualism. Thus, the Church is transformed from a place of meeting and communion with God into a wall which separates God from man. Wherever this spirit rules, it brings on the removal of the charismatic aspect of Church and quenches the Spirit of God who holds it together and directs it. There is always a serious danger of quenching the Spirit of God in a particular local Church and for this Church to cease to exist, as so very many churches known from antiquity have ceased to exist.

When the Church loses its real essence and changes into a simple social institution, it is not at all indestructible. The Church is indestructible and eternal only as the communion of God with mass. This Church has existed, exists, and will exist until the completion of the age: "and the gates of hell will not prevail against it" (Mt 16.18). The several churches, though, and Christians severally, belong then and share only in the indestructible truth of the Church when they belong to God and participate in the grace of the Holy Spirit, when they try to live as real victors over death and as truly free men. Therefore, true freedom cannot exist elsewhere, but only in the Church, in the union, that is, and the communion of man with God. When a Christian ceases to live as a free man, he ceases essentially to be a Christian. And when one is not a true Christian, he cannot be a really free man.

However, the way in which Christianity is interpreted, and especially the way in which it is represented within the world, often provokes in men a completely different impression. It is natural that many misunderstandings are created. In this case, what God said of the Israelites by the mouth of the Prophet Isaiah is also valid for Christians: "Through you, my name is blasphemed among the nations" (Is 52.5).

Unfortunately, this phenomenon is not rare. Men often appear who deny God and hold the Church in contempt in the name of their freedom. But the freedom which leads man to transcend himself without joining him to the source of freedom, God, is self-destructive and simultaneously destructive for man. Freedom which is not a fruit of truth is the smell of death. In the final analysis, the denial of God is the denial of freedom. When man thinks that he can deny God as his Lord, in essence he is denying the possibility of transcending himself, that is, his own freedom. As the contemporary philosopher Karl Jaspers has observed,

> The more authentically free a man is, the greater his certainty of God. When I am authentically free, I am certain that I am not free through myself.[3]

Man's real liberator is God himself, and true freedom is a gift of the Holy Spirit: "Where the Spirit of the Lord is, there is freedom" (2 Cor 3.17).

Nicholas Kabasilas: The Life in Christ 2 (Extract)[4]

The baptismal washing renders us pure of every habit and action of sin in that it makes us partakers of Christ's life-giving health.

Since we share in his resurrection through the baptismal washing Christ gives us another life, and forms members and provides the faculties needed by those who attain to the life to come. It is for this reason that I am completely released from the indictments and forthwith receive health, particularly because it is entirely the work of God who cannot be subject to time.

Further, it is not merely at this present time that he benefits our race, as though he needed time, but he has already done so. It is not now that the Master is paying the penalty for the sins which I have committed, or preparing the cure and forming the members and providing the faculties, but he has already done so. It was when he mounted the cross and died and rose again that the freedom of mankind came about, that the form and the beauty were created and the new members were prepared. All, then, that is needed now is to approach and draw near to the gifts.

This is what the baptismal washing accomplishes for us. It brings the dead to life, the captives to freedom, the mutilated it provides with the blessed form. The ransom has already been paid; now we are merely being released. The Chrism has been poured forth and its sweet odor encompasses everything; all that remains is to breathe it. Or rather, not even the breathing remains for us, since the ability to breathe it has been prepared by the Savior, as well as the possibility of being released and enlightened. By coming into the world he not merely rose as its Light, but even provided the eye to see it. He not merely poured forth the chrism but even gave the means of perceiving it. This sacred washing joins our organs and faculties to those who have been washed. Like formless and shapeless matter we go down into this water; in it we meet with the form that is beautiful.

That is why all blessings arise for us at the same time. They were prepared for us beforehand, as is said, "Behold, I have made ready my dinner, my oxen and my fat calves are killed, and everything is ready; come to the marriage feast" (Mt 22.4). This alone is lacking at the feast — that those who have been invited should come.

In the case of those who come, what more is needed for happiness? Nothing whatever. In the world to come we shall come to Christ duly prepared, but now, having approached him, we are being prepared. At that time we must have all things in order so that we may approach him, but now those who approach must receive all things. It is for this reason that the foolish virgins will not then be able to come to the bridal chamber, while in the present age he calls the unwise to the feasting and the toasts of friendship. Then it will be impossible for the dead to revive, for the blind to see, and the deformed to be formed anew. In this present life only the will and the eagerness are needed and all things follow, for he says, "I came into the world that they might have life" (Jn 10.10), and "I have come as light into the world" (Jn 12.46).

It is of this ineffable loving-kindness that he has accomplished all things by which we have been released. He left something for us to contribute to our freedom — that we should believe that by Baptism we have salvation and that we should willingly approach it, so that from thence everything should be imputed to us, and that gratitude should be due for the things by which he has benefited us. Whenever, then, it happens that those who have been washed straightway depart this life and bring with them nothing out the seat of Baptism, he calls them to their crowns as though they had striven for the kingdom.

NOTES

[1] *To the Smyrnaeans* 5.1.
[2] Saint Maximos Confessor, *Scholia on the Divine Names* 4.33, PG 4.308.
[3] *Way to Wisdom,* tr. Ralph Manheim (New Haven, 1979), p. 65.
[4] Tr. C. J. deCatanzaro (Crestwood, 1974), pp. 78-80.

CHAPTER SIXTEEN

Deification

Aristotle in his *Politics* interprets the greed of man and the endless number of his inquiries, noting: "The nature of desire is infinite, but the majority of people live to fulfill it."[1] The whole world is too poor to be able to satisfy human desire. This is becoming more obvious today as man extends his conquests beyond the earth, but without feeling thereby more complete or more happy. On the contrary, one can observe that man's conquests are increasing his inquiries still more and the satisfaction of his desires is making his greed more intense.

This phenomenon, which can be considered a paradox for a materialistic anthropological theory, is not only intelligible, but also perfectly natural for Christian anthropology. Man, according to Christian teaching, is a creature "in the image and likeness" of God (Gen

1.26). This means that he has marks of the divine in his nature. The infinite, the perfect, the eternal, and all the marks that characterize the uncreated and transcendent God are reflected in some way in created and finite men. Thus, the paradox is not to be found in the desires and inquiries of man, but in his very nature and structure. The paradox is not that man desires the infinite, the perfect, the eternal, but that, being a created and perishable existence, he cannot be fulfilled if he is not led to what he desires, if he is not deified.

The longing for deification is innate in man. Man is fulfilled by this longing and by it he is led to value and realize the goal of his existence. As Saint Maximos Confessor observes,

> God made us so that we might become 'partakers of the divine nature' (2 Pt 1.4) and sharers in his eternity, and so that we might come to be like him (cf. 1 Jn 3.2) through deification by grace.[1]

But on the other hand, the longing for deification destroys man and leads him into perversion and madness. This longing led man into original sin. It lies essentially at the base of every human activity which establishes and perpetuates the fall. In the "Doxastikon of the Orthros" for the Feast of the Annunciation of the Mother of God, the hymnography of the Orthodox Church notes the following:

> In ancient time Adam was deceived:
> he sought to become God,
> but he did not receive his desire.
> Now God becomes man,
> that he might make Adam good.

God became man in order to deify man: "For he became man that we might become god."[3] In the person of Christ, human nature has been deified and a new root has been created, which is in a position to transmit life and incorruptibility to all its shoots. The faithful who are enrolled in the body of Christ become sharers in the grace and life of God. And so, what was impossible and inaccessible for man has become possible and accessible to him through the God-man. Christ as the God-man had the entire "fulness of divinity" (Col

2.9) and "from his fulness, we have all received" (Jn 1.16).[4]

But the incarnation of God, which made possible the deification of man, could not be realized except with the co-operation of man. The flesh, which the Son and Word of God received by his incarnation, derived from his most holy Mother. Thus, the Holy Virgin co-operated in the work of God's incarnation by lending to Christ his flesh. As Mother of Christ, she is mother and lady and mistress of all men who share in the body of Christ and become members of his Church.

> Therefore, by this, the Mother of God is mistress and queen and lady and mother of all the saints. All the saints are her servants for she is Mother of God; they are her sons, for they have communicated in the spotless flesh of her Son.[5]

Hence, the Orthodox Church honors the Holy Virgin as the cause of "the deification of all."[6] And finally, from the moral point of view, the Blessed Virgin is the first to walk the way of deification in her perfect humility and obedience. Her self-offering to the will of God — "Behold the servant of God; may it happen to me in accordance with your word" (Lk 1.38) — constituted the condition for the conception and birth of Christ. Everyone who wants to receive Christ within him is called to offer himself unreservedly to God, imitating the humility and obedience of the Blessed Virgin. This made Saint Gregory Palamas propose the Blessed Virgin as our example in the course of our journey to deification.[7]

The deification of man, then, presupposes his willing self-offering to God. As man offers himself to Christ, as he combats his individual will in order that the will of God be realized, as he puts his self-love to death so that God and his neighbor (who is the image of God) might live in him, he co-operates in his personal deification. He co-operates in this essential transformation of his existence, which is realized within the body of Christ, the Church, by the grace of the Holy Spirit. And so, the Christian conquers in Christ decay and death. He changes what is forced into what is willed and "assumes the nature by his assent, becoming dead to the world of his own accord."[8]

A certain staretz, who was asked a little before his death if he was going to die, said, "I have not yet learned humility,"[9] He saw that he did not possess the spirit of the unrestricted humility of Christ. Perfection in humility is perfection along the road to confront death; it is perfection in the journey to deification in Christ.

> We must all pass through the mystery of death, in order to live a fuller likeness to Christ. Our God and Father leads us over this threshold, which is still unknown to us, into the light of unending day.[10]

The egoistic making of man into god is the opposite of deification in Christ. While deification in Christ assumes humility and self-offering, this egoistic making of man into god is founded on self-assurance and conceit. It is an act which is pursued with the natural possibilities and abilities of man or with his moral and spiritual development. But man cannot offer himself anything which he does not have. Nor is he in a position to produce something which transcends his nature. Man is and remains created and mortal. Therefore, even the "god-making" which he pursues moves within the limits of death and is given the lie by death. But in spite of all this, man usually prefers the latter because it doesn't require the renunciation of the ego.

Deification, which is defined in the areopagitic texts as "assimilation and union with God, so far as is possible,"[11] is granted as a gift of the uncreated God to created man. As Saint Maximos Confessor observes, "we passively experience deification by grace as something which is above nature, but we do not actively accomplish it; for by nature we do not have the capacity to attain deification," and "created things are not by nature able to accomplish deification . . ."[12] The deification of man is the work of the one Triadic God. God assumes man in Christ by the grace of the Holy Spirit and leads him to the glory of his kingdom. This event is revealed in the life of Christ and especially in his Transfiguration and Ascension.

The Transfiguration of Christ holds a central position in Orthodox theology and worship. A correct consideration of it has capital im-

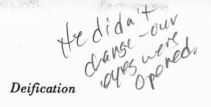

portance for a correct understanding of the Orthodox Church's teaching about the nature of the deification of man. The transfiguration of Christ according to the tradition of Orthodoxy was not realized by some temporary change in his person or by the assumption of a special brightness which he did not have previously, but by the disciples becoming capable of seeing — and even then only partially — the natural glory of his divinity which existed from the beginning in his divine-human hypostasis. Saint John of Damascus writes characteristically the following:

> It was not what he had not assumed, but what he had seemed to his own disciples to be that was changed by his opening their eyes and making those who were blind to see. This is the "he was changed before them." For now he was seen different in appearance to what he seemed before, though he maintained his identity.[13]

Besides, with the ascension of Christ, the work of God's economy and of man's deification was made complete. The ascension of Christ, like his entire earthly life, is not his private affair, but reveals the destiny and character of renewed man:

> For what he became, Christ became for us . . . and the life he lived, he lived for us . . . and he was raised for us and assumed into heaven, in advance providing for us the resurrection to endless ages and our assumption.[14]

The ascension of Christ frees human nature from universal necessity and raises it to the glory of God the Father by the grace of the Holy Spirit. "God has made us alive in Christ, we who were dead in our sins . . . and has raised us with him and made us sit with him in the heavenly places" (Eph 2.4-6).

According to the teaching of the Scriptures and of the Fathers of the Church, Christ is the cause and recapitulation of creation: "all things were made through him and for him" (Col 1.16). Analysing this passage, Saint Nicholas Kabasilas observes:

> It was for the new man that human nature was created at the

beginning, and for him mind and desire were prepared. Our reason we have received in order that we may know Christ, our desire in order that we might hasten to him. We have memory in order that we may carry him in us, since he himself is the Archetype for those who are created. It was not the old Adam who was the model for the new, but the new Adam for the old.[15]

In Christ, then, is found man's worth. Every human inquiry is, in the end, a christological inquiry, in spite of all its differentiations and variations, in spite of failures and distortions. Man seeks Christ with his mind and his desire, with his memory and his imagination. But like Adam, every one who seeks to satisfy and give value to his existence after the pattern of Adam is frustrated in his desire and, instead of becoming worthy, he becomes distorted. Only in Christ is found man's value, as well as the value of the entire world. In the body of Christ, the Church, man and the entire world find the purpose of their existence again.

The deification of man, then, is not a private matter for him, nor does it move only in the vertical dimension of his relations with God. Deification is realized in the framework of his life in communion within the Church. Thus it also comprises the horizontal dimension of man's life, that is, his relations with his fellow men and the world. God, to whose life deified man shares, is not an "individuality," but the consubstantial and undivided Trinity of persons.[16] The image of God which is engraved in man is not limited to the individual hypostasis, but extends to his entire nature and covers all his interpersonal and social relations. Thus, deification does not constitute an accomplishment or privilege of the individual, but an ecclesiological event. Deification is a fruit of the perfection of the faithful as members of the body of Christ, the Church, which is therefore called "communion of deification."[17]

The communion of deification is not a system of principle or constitutions or of some objective or objectified values. The communion of deification is a communion of persons. As a communion of persons, it is a communion of love and freedom. It is a communion of absolute offering and absolute fulness in the image of and by participation in the Triadic Divinity. Here, the person is not placed against the whole, and the whole does not suppress the person. This offering does not reduce the fulness, because it forms a constitutive element of it. The fulness is not created by quantity, because it does not constitute a collective magnitude. The one exists in the many and the many in the one.

The consubstantial and undivided Trinity assumes man into its glory by love and philanthropy, "that there might be," as Saint Theophilos of Antioch writes characteristically, "God, Word, Wisdom, man."[18] In this divine-human communion, the basic and only difference in the end which separates God from man is not abolished, that is the difference between uncreated and created. God is and remains uncreated. Man is and remains created. But the uncreated God who assumed and deified created human nature in Christ, assumes and deifies every human person by the grace of the Holy Spirit, including him in the communion of deification. Thus, what was given to human nature in Christ is offered to every human person who receives Christ and lives as a member of his body. Man becomes a friend of God and similar to Christ. But while Christ is "God by nature" and "man by (God's) goodness," man remains man "by nature" and becomes "God by grace."[19]

The deification of man, like the Church which declares the good news of the communion of deification within history, has an escatological character. The fulness of deification is revealed by the transition "from the grace which is in faith to the grace of vision,"[20] wherever God is seen, "face to face" (1 Cor 13.12). But already during the period of "grace in faith," which is the time of the present life, experiences of the "grace by vision" are granted to the faithful. As Saint John the Evangelist writes:

> we are now children of God, and it has not yet been shown what we shall be; we know that if it is shown, we will be like him, because we shall see him as he is (1 Jn 3.2).

The view that the faithful can maintain the grace of the Holy Spirit during his present life "unknowingly" and "without perceiving" is characterized by Saint Symeon the New Theologian as malicious and blasphemous. So he notes, then, if the graces of the Holy Spirit

> ... act in us without our being conscious of it, without our feeling
> anything of them, it is obvious that we will not receive this feeling
> at all even in the eternal life which follows from them (i.e. the graces
> of the Holy Spirit) and remains in us, nor will we see the light of
> the Holy Spirit. But we will remain dead and blind and insensible
> then as now. And so our hope becomes vain, according to them, and
> our way pointless, since we are in death and have not received any
> sensation of eternal life.[21]

The sensation of the glory of God begins in the present life and
presupposes the purity of man's heart, inasmuch as, Christ says, the
"pure in heart" shall see God (Mt 5.8), it is natural that where there
is purity the vision of God should follow.

> In any case, when purity occurs, contemplation follows with it. For
> if purity exists here, vision is here also; if you say that you will have
> the vision of God after death, you put purity after death and thus
> you will not be able ever to see God, since no way exists for you
> to find purity after death.[22]

Participation in the glory of God transfigures man. The iron which
is heated in the fire, as the Fathers note, becomes and is called fire,
without ceasing to be iron. And the man who shares in the divine
light becomes and is called light, without ceasing to be man. The
whole of man becomes deiform. The uncreated God dwells and is
active in created human nature and, therefore, the deified man is
not proud of his virtues and good works. His every good work and
his every virtue is finally a fruit of the grace of God who is active
in him.[23]

By grace, deified man receives anything that the uncreated God
has.[24] And so he lives an unlimited and unending perfection. God
is infinite and the possibilities for man's development are infinite.
The grace of God is unlimited, and the blessedness of the faithful
who participates in it is unlimited.[25] As a friend of God and god by
grace, he is freed from space and time. He becomes

... without beginning and without end, no longer bearing in himself the agitated life of time which has a beginning and an end, nor disturbed by many passions, but only the divine and eternal life of the indwelling Word, which no death can end.[26]

Thus, the deification of man, which is begun by the deification of his nature in the person of Christ, is completed by the offering of this gift to every human person. This offering is initiated by the grace of the Holy Spirit during the present life and is revealed in its fulness in the future life. The person is not charged into an arithmetic unit to promote the whole, but is steemed as a unique and unrepeatable value. The whole fulness is offered and revealed in the person, and the fulness exists and acts personally. This is the witness and the gift of the Triadic God.

All that is mine is yours and yours is mine . . . and I have given them the glory that you gave me, that they may be one as we are one, I in them and you in me, that they may be completely one (Jn 17.10,22-23).

The effort which aims to make man into god is found in precisely the opposite direction. This effort pursues divinization by collectivization. Fulness is not taken as an offering. Therefore, it is sought as the arithmetic conclusion of all the possible factors. The person is used as an arithmetic unit to promote the whole. And the apotheosis of the whole cannot be located anywhere else than where the independence and particularity of the person vanish. It is the direction and spirit of "giantism" and totalitarianism, to which our civilization is enslaved.

This titanic effort to make a god of man has reached in our days a frightening impasse. By alienating the human person and changing it into a simple number and anonymous accessory to an intricate, impersonal and uncontrollable machine, it is already directing the entire world to general alienation and ruin. The idol to which man has sacrificed his person is tending to tear our whole species apart. Before this fearful impasse, the Church repeats firmly and unalterably its eternal proclamation of the deification of man in Christ: Deification, which is not realized by abolition of the person, but by giving him absolute value as an image of God, in which the infinite, without beginning, and endless, truth of God's life and existence is manifest, deification, which is realized always in communion with the other members of the Church in the image of God in Trinity.

Saint Gregory Palamas
Homily 53.37-41, "On the Presentation
of the Mother of God"[27]

37. Thus, (the Blessed Virgin) alone is the boundary of the created and uncreated natures, and no one comes to God except through her and the mediator born from her. Nor is any gift of God given, except through her, whether it be to angels or men. For as, to take the example of lampstands on earth made of glass or something else transparent, it is not possible to look at a light or to share in the rays from it, except by means of the lampstand, so it is impossible for anyone to gaze up to God and progress by himself toward anything at all, except through this truly God-bearing and divinely shining lampstand, the ever Virgin Mary. "For God is in the midst of her, and she shall not be moved" (Ps 45.5), it says.

38. If, then, the return is in accord with the measure of love for God, whoever loves the Son is loved by him and his Father and becomes an abode for both to inhabit and dwell mystically in the soul, in accord with the Master's promise. Who could love him more than his mother, who not only gave birth to him alone but also alone conceived without intercourse? And so her love is twofold in nature, since no husband shared that love. Who could be loved more than the mother by her only son, who proceeded from her alone ineffably in the last days, as he proceeded from the Father alone before the ages? How could the honor due her not be compounded through this fitting arrangement by him who descended to fulfill the law? If the love of the Father and the Son is one and the honor and union from both of these is also from the Spirit (O the graces of the Virgin, surpassing understandingly!), she bears all the uncreated Trinity within her soul, in whose womb the one was conceived without seed, and she being a virgin gave birth without sin.

39. As, then, he journeyed to us through her alone — he who was invisible to all before her "appeared on earth and associated with men" (Baruch 3.37) — so also all progress during the next unceasing age in the divine illumination and all revelation of the most divine mysteries and every idea of spiritual gifts is incomprehensible to anyone without her. She is the first to receive the fulness of him who fills all, and she renders it discernible to all, distributing appropriately to each in the proportion and measure of the purity of each. Thus, she is the treasury and governor of the wealth of divinity.

The highest cherubic hierarchies look to her and trust her. As much as they all desire to be bound to her with an uplifting effort, so much more they desire that illumination be shed through her and the divine graces be distributed and that those spiritual powers under them may all share proportionately in the divine love and the divine dawning that occurs through her. The status and the clarity of divine illumination will follow for us and divine desire, their immaterial and unceasing love, and their highest and sincere inclination for this truly deiform Virgin.

40. Since this is the eternal order in heaven, that the lesser share through the greater in the structure of being above (and the Virgin Mother is incomparably the greatest of all) those who participate in God, do so through her and those who know God shall know her as the locale of the uncontainable. Those who sing praise to God, shall sing praise to her with God. She is the cause of what was before her, the guardian of what is after her, and the agent of eternal things. She is the subject of the prophets, the beginning of the Apostles, the strengthening of the martyrs, the foundation of the teachers. She is the glory of those on earth, the delight of those in heaven, the adornment of all creation. She is the beginning, source, and root of secret goods. She is the summit and perfection of everything holy.

41. O holy Virgin, how shall I express all to you? How shall I fulfill my desire? How shall I glorify you, the treasury of glory? Just your memory has sanctified the one who desires you. Only inclining to you has made my mind more clear, raising it straight to the divine height. The eye of my understanding is made clear in you. In you the spirit shines with the visitation of the Holy Spirit. You have become the treasury and place of graces, not in order to seize them for yourself,

but to fill everything with grace. For the treasurer of inexhaustible treasures is the trustee for the sake of distribution. What could your wealth do if it were locked up, since it does not diminish? Give to us richly, then, Lady, and if we cannot contain it, increase our capacity and so measure out still more. You alone have not received my measure, for everything has been given into your hand.

NOTES

[1] *Politics* B, 1267b,3-5.

[2] *Various Texts* 1.42, *Philokalia* 2,173.

[3] Saint Athanasios, *On the Incarnation* 54.3, PG 25.192B.

[4] Saint Gregory Palamas makes the following relevant note: "Who among those created would be able to contain all the omnipotent strength of the Spirit, except the one who was conceived in the virgin womb, by the presence of the Holy Spirit and the overshadowing of the power of the Most High? And so, he contained 'all the fulness of divinity' and 'we have all received of his fulness.' " *Triads in Defence of the Holy Hesychasts* 3.1.34, *Erga* 2, 630.

[5] Saint Symeon the New Theologian, *Ethical Treatises* 1.10.166-70. J. Darrouzès (ed.), *Traités theologiques et éthiques*, vol. 1, "Sources Chretiennes" 22 (Paris, 1966), p. 264.

[6] Canon of the *Akathist Hymn*, Ode 6, 1st Troparion.

[7] See especially *Homily* 51, "On the Entrance of the Mother of God," *Erga* 11,230ff.

[8] Saint Maximos Confessor, *On the Lord's Prayer*, PG 90.904A.

[9] Archimandrite Sophrony, *The Monk of Mount Athos*, tr. Rosemary Edmonds (Crestwood, 1975), p. 121.

[10] Archimandrite Sophrony, *Voir Dieu tel qu'il est* (Genève, 1984), p. 82. This passage seems not to appear in the ET cited above which is based on an earlier French edition; but cf. p. 89ff.

[11] Ps-Dionysios Areopagite, *On the Ecclesiastical Hierarchy*, 5,3, PG 3.376A.

[12] *Various Texts* 1.75-76, *Philokalia* 2,181-2.

[13] *First Homily on the Transfiguration* 12, PG 96.564C.

[14] Saint Gregory Palamas, *Homily* 21.4, *Erga* 10,26.

[15] *The Life in Christ* 6.12, p. 190.

[16] Saint Maximos Confessor comments in this regard: "Note that what pertains to the Holy Trinity is united in communion." *Scholia on the Divine Names* 2.1, PG 4.213A.

[17] Saint Gregory Palamas, *Demonstrative Discourse* 2.78. *Erga* 1.149.

[18] *To Autolykos* 2.15.

[19]Saint Symeon the New Theologian, *Ethical Treatises* 10.731-33, J. Darrouzès (ed.) *Traités théologiques et éthiques,* "Sources Chretiennes" 129 (Paris, 1966), p. 312.

[20]Saint Maximos Confessor, *The Church's Mystagogy* 24, *Selected Writings,* tr. George C. Berthold (New York, 1985), p. 207.

[21]*Ethical Treatises* 10.508-16, J. Darrouzes (ed.) *Traités théologiques et éthiques,* "Sources Chretiennes" 129 (Paris, 1966), p. 296.

[22]*Ethical Treatises* 5.115-25, J. Darrouzès (ed.) *Traités théologiques et éthiques,* 1, "Sources Chrétiennes" 129 (Paris, 1966), p. 88.

[23]"For every kind of virtue comes to us if God is active in us." Saint Gregory Palamas, *Homily* 33.7, *Erga* 10,338.

[24]"The man deified by grace is everything that God is except for identity of essence." Saint Maximos Confessor, *To Thalassios* 61.16, PG 90.44D.

[25]Saint Gregory of Nyssa, *The Life of Moses,* PG 44.404A.

[26]Saint Maximos Confessor, *On Doubts,* PG 91.1144C.

[27]*Erga,* 11, 308-14.

Bibliography

Holy Transfiguration Monastery, *The Ascetical Homilies of Saint Isaac the Syrian* (Boston: Holy Transfiguration Monastery, 1984).

Krivochéine, Abp. B. *In the Light of Christ.* tr. Anthony Gythiel, (Crestwood: St. Vladimir's Press, 1981).

Lossky, V. *In the Image and Likeness of God.* ed. John H. Erickson and Thomas E. Bird (Crestwood: St. Vladimir's Press, 1974).

Lossky, V. *The Mystical Theology of the Eastern Church* (Crestwood: St. Vladimir's Press, 1974).

Lossky, V. *Orthodox Theology.* tr. Ian and Ihita Kesarcodi-Watson (Crestwood: St. Vladimir's Press, 1978).

Lossky, V. *The Vision of God.* tr. Asheleigh Moorhouse (Leighton Buzzard, 1973).

Mantzaridis, G. *The Deification of Man.* tr. Liaidain Sherrard (Crestwood: St. Vladimir's Press, 1984).

Mantzaridis, G. *Sociology of Christianity* (Thessalonike: Regopoulos, 1990).

Meyendorff, J. *Saint Gregory Palamas and Orthodox Spirituality* (Crestwood: St. Vladimir's Press, 1977).

A Monk of the Eastern Church. *On the Invocation of the Name of Jesus* (London, 1949).

A Monk of the Eastern Church. *Orthodox Spirituality* (London, 1974).

A Monk of the Eastern Church. *The Jesus Prayer* (Crestwood: St. Vladimir's Press, 1987).

Nellas, P. *Deification in Christ.* tr. Norman Russell (Crestwood: St. Vladimir's Press, 1987).

Schmemann, A. *For the Life of the World.* (Crestwood: St. Vladimir's Press, 1973).

Schmemann, A. *Great Lent* (Crestwood: St. Vladimir's Press, 1974).

Schmemann, A. *Of Water and the Spirit* (Crestwood: St. Vladimir's Press, 1974).

Sophrony, Archimandrite. *The Monk of Mount Athos.* tr. Rosemary Edmonds (Crestwood: St. Vladimir's Press, 1975).

Sophrony, Archimandrite. *Wisdom from Mount Athos.* tr. Rosemary Edmonds (Crestwood: St. Vladimir's Press, 1975).

Sophrony, Archimandrite. *His Life is Mine.* tr. Rosemary Edmonds (Crestwood: St. Vladimir's Press, 1977).

Staniloae, D. *The Mystagogy of Saint Maximos the Confessor* (Athens, 1973.

Vaporis, N. M. *Father Kosmas: The Apostle to the Poor* (Brookline: Holy Cross Orthodox Press, 1974).

Vasileios, Archimandrite. *Hymn of Entry.* tr. Elizabeth Briere (Crestwood: St. Vladimir's Press, 1984).

Ware, T. *The Orthodox Way* (Harmondsworth, 1967).

Ware, T. *The Power of the Name.* 2nd ed. (Oxford, 1986).

Weber, M. *The Protestant Ethic and the Spirit of Capitalism* (London, 1985).

Index of Names

Made in the USA